Atlas of Darkness

Kori Hagel

Atlas of Darkness

Printed by Create Space, an Amazon company

ISBN-13: 9781977904119
ISBN-10: 1977904114

Cover art Kori Hagel
Photographer: Tegan Jay Photography

Edition: November 2017

dedicated to the benevolence of Mother Earth:
Thank you for strengthening me through your power of divine feminine.

and with immense gratitude to my therapist:
It was with your unconditional support that I was able to access my
highest wisdom from within. The space you held for me was my anchor
on my darkest nights. I will forever be grateful for this gift.

For my mother,
Donna

Dear Reader:
This work of truth comprises three parts.

1. *The Pain In The Darkness.*
2. *Night Vision: Trusting The Darkness.*
3. *All The Love: The Divinity in the Darkness.*

Part One covers my life before surrender. It reveals murky depths; eye opening for some readers, familiar to others.

Part Two—post surrender—offers my rise to the surface, an emergence into the life I live now. The premise is that, in knowing my past, you will find a way to come to terms with yours so that you can embrace the present.

Part Three shares approaches, practices, and techniques that shape my days and comfort my nights; it offers opportunities to discover possibilities for your own healing. These 'menus of self-love' will be varied, doable, and result oriented.

Facing my darkness was the hardest thing I have ever done. I wholeheartedly believe it almost killed me. With conviction, I now believe in the divinity of darkness; nourishment and lessons for my soul that only the darkness could teach.

I denied, detoured, and dodged real life for a long time. Blind to how avoidance caused more pain than dealing with things.

At that time I did not appreciate the sweetness of surrender, nor did I comprehend the authenticity of my true self. I thought my emotions were wrong, and that surrender meant giving up. Of course, thoughts, when they are thought over and over, become beliefs.

Many of my visions of my darkest days echo the story of Alice's Wonderland— the similarities are interesting and disturbing. Much like the rabbit hole Lewis Carroll created, I had my own hole in the ground that I called my soul swamp; the bottom of which was a mucky pool of still, skank mud.

From the bottom of the swamp I could look up and see the light of day, but the walls were slippery. Impossible to climb. From this prison of sorts, I spent a lot of my days fiercely determined to scale the walls but, like a hamster on a wheel, I got nowhere fast.

Climb. Slide. Panic. Repeat.

I thought I could use my determination and smarts to read my way past the pain—rather than facing it, without the concept of surrendering—and emerge from the swamp with a kind of trophy. I read every self-help book I could find and performed for my therapist regularly, but I never 'leaned into the pain'. I worked my program to 'win'. A 'give me the information I need to end the pain as fast as possible so I can get the fuck out'. But, with that mentality, I became mired in the thickest mud at the bottom and, for a brief time, the swamp swallowed me whole.

Discomfort was my security blanket. Drama was my addiction. Both played an integral role in keeping dysfunction alive.

My reality, at the time, was demented, damaging, abusive, and volatile. Lost, self-hating, and faithless, I reacted with anger, drama, substance abuse, and participation in dysfunctional relationships—specifically one long-term partnership.

My coping techniques verged on dangerous. Unable to admit that the relationship was abusive, I became obsessed over fixing it, compulsively so.

And in that hellish dark relationship, I finally shattered; a mere shell of a human, questioning my faith and worthiness. Unbelievable as it may seem to 'the balanced and seemingly sane' it still took all of my might to leave. And it took something beyond a super-power to summon and grant forgiveness.

In those days I ran a lot; even won my first race while in that relationship. It was the perfect representation of outrunning my shadow. Hemingway couldn't have crafted a better metaphor. Eventually, an injury stopped me from physically running, which, in turn, forced me to stop running emotionally.

Suicide whispered in my ear, daily.

The only remaining option was to lie at the bottom of the swamp and surrender. And in that submission I would learn the lessons my soul needed.

At the base of the swamp, I reclined on a bright pink floaty, and stared up past the black walls to the tiny opening of light. I spent over a year-and-a-half there. Time well spent.

In the swamp I learned the divinity of being where I was at. I learned the holiness of slowing down. I learned the sacred art of crying. And, more importantly, I learned to stop labeling and justifying my emotions. I learned to honor where my heart is at. In essence, the environment in the swamp taught me things about the earth, and I learned how to garden. From a vine of Anguish—and almost suffocating from its rapid growth of poisonous leaves—I learned that not all roots are toxic.

I developed tools and daily rituals. An emergency list. I learned deep self-care through the crafting of foods. I learned to fiercely protect my inner child. I learned that I am useless to the world if I am not in a selfishly divine state of self-care. And I was able to use those skills, proving that the rituals are essential for surviving unanticipated blackouts that life throws our way.

If I do not show up for me first,
I suck at showing up for other humans, and for my life purpose.

I believe the fundamental truth to fulfillment is divine selfishness; the first step to self-love.

When we intimately take care of our own heart—our garden—only then can we extend productive care to the rest of the world. Only self-loving humans show up for other humans with their full potential.

I intend for my story to illuminate even the most tortured of lives, and offer a path to a safe place where each can sow seeds of self under the moonlight, nurture her garden, and harvest a new-self.

Table of Contents

Part One

The Pain In The Darkness

CHAPTER 1

Sixth Sense
1984-1990

MY MUM SAYS that my arrival on February 12, 1984, was like a breath of fresh air—a healthy baby to ease the emotional burden she'd felt for two-and-a-half years due to my older brother's disability and his tenuous hold on life.

I was six months old when he passed away during complications experienced in heart surgery. He was three years old.

There are many studies relating to the age children form and retain memories. What I believe is that a person of any age only needs to be present to experience something which manifests deep within. Whether or not that defines memory is irrelevant; I know my brother imprinted on my soul the same way a migrating bird knows her flight path.

What each of us knows is a unique blend of what we recall and what we have been told. The combination of all our senses, added to a genetic recipe, along with circumstance and experience, produces individuality.

Through Jamie's relocation to the space of angels, I became the eldest child, by default, assuming the role of the not-really-first-born to a sister and twin brothers. Mum's theory is that I developed emotionally and physically faster than most because she was busy with Jamie.

I was a messy and adventurous child. Most early photos show me covered in mud; always a dirty face and a distended belly that one imagines a preschool Buddha might have had—a round tummy filled with the happiness and innocence of an early childhood of chasing ducks, building snowmen, and riding horses.

Ours was a busy household—albums filled with snapshots of candles on cakes, children on laps, and large groups squeezed into the lens evidence this—but never too busy for laughter, love, and bedtime tuck-ins. Mum looked after the four of us, and Dad went to work. Grammy (Mum's mom) and Grandma (Dad's mom), and extended family were often nearby. I twirled about in the center of it all, dancing in the chaos. Always dancing. And, along with the love of a good mother, my greatest security of all was that I was loved unconditionally by a man who, while he watched the television show M*A*S*H, tickled the back of his daughter who lay on the floor in front of him. The kind of guy you up your game for in Kindergarten by putting extra sparkles on Father's Day creations.

We were the Once Upon a Time family, complete with camping equipment—Mum, Dad, Daughters, and Twin-sons—well on our way to Happily Ever After.

"Good Night, Sweet Dreams, God Bless, I love you". I clearly remember those words. Mum and Dad said them every night to us. This particular night, during my sixth summer, we were camping in British Columbia.

When I woke in the morning, there was a hole in the window of the trailer. The shape of the break and its spatial relationship to the table became a permanent frame in my mind. My parents weren't there. My Aunt and Uncle had magically appeared. A cousin as well. It hadn't been planned that they'd join our summer holiday.

My day carried on kind of 'normal' except that other campers asked me what had happened in the night. Why the emergency vehicles? I told them I didn't know about anything happening in the night.

Later, there was a call made from a payphone. We were, meaning my Aunt, Uncle, and/or Cousin, on the line with my Mum, who was at a hospital. She told 'us', through the phone, that all of Dad's organs were shutting down, and that we could not go and see him, and that he was going to die.'

I prayed on my black rosary—a necklace of prayer beads—like no other six year old had ever prayed.

We didn't get to see him at the hospital.

We didn't get to see him ever again.

My prayers were not answered.

※▬◎ ◎▬※

I have no clue how my Mum got through it. Is that what is meant by the strength and grace of a Mother?

Apparently he'd complained of a bad headache, sat down at the trailer's table, and lost consciousness; his head hit the window. There was a blood vessel inside him that was like a balloon. This is called an aneurism. That night it ruptured. That's when he lost consciousness, his weight breaking the pane of glass. Really, the window doesn't matter, but I remember that frame and broken glass as clearly as I remember brushing my teeth this morning. He passed away July 10, 1990.

CHAPTER 2

Seven, Eight, Seeds of Hate
1990-1992

WHEN WE ARRIVED home in Calgary, after my Dad had died from a blood vessel that was blown up like a balloon and then exploded in his head, I was still six years old, but not the same carefree child.

In a state of bewilderment I have no memory if we flew or drove home. Either way, when we pulled up at our house, I refused to get out of the red truck. I might as well have been a child watching her village burn to the ground so filled with rage was I; wanting to destroy those who had burned it. Unknowingly, I initiated a vendetta.

My Mum sent her eldest brother, my Uncle Bob—my buddy—to try to reason with me.

When he approached the truck, I jumped out of the truck and ran into the bushes.

**"After your father's passing,
you never looked at people the same way again,"
he once told me.**

My Mum was left with four children. She and I had an extremely close connection. I sort-of took on role of the 'man' by her side. Of course, that was never her intention, but it is one I assumed since there were three younger siblings toddling about. I was protective of these humans I called my family members.

I remember countless nights breaking down, having long and tearful conversations with Mum. She would come and tuck me in, and we would reminisce, crying and hugging: being in pain together.

She was wonderful; always had wisdom beyond her years. I searched for answers—where my Dad was, whether or not heaven exists—and she did her best to explain. But no matter how wise she was, she could not give me what I wanted.

I wanted my Dad.

And

I missed him. She missed him. His mother missed him. Her mother missed him. The entire immediate and extended family, and his friends, missed him. They all appeared to deal with it appropriately. I didn't.

I lacked the experience needed to process and survive tragedy, loss, and heart-wrenching sadness that a mother of four children—five, if you count my brother, which I do—possessed.

I was a child who had just formed a trust in the world, old enough to recognize life then watch it shatter into a hundred-thousand pieces. Too young to have the knowledge to analyze my situation and come up with a rational response—heck, I didn't even swear yet; I'd only had a little more than 80 months on this planet. Not even 2500 days.

Measure that against the full maturity of a 36,500 day full lifetime.

There is no right time to lose a father. But six, for me, was a pivotal developmental stage.

"Give me a child until he is seven and I will show you the man."

~ **Aristotle**

The philosopher's point is that who we are at around age seven is our blueprint for the future.

I stopped letting people into my heart at six.

One day, when Grammy (my Mum's Mum) was trying to punish me for something, I carried a tray of ice cubes and raced up the stairs as she gave chase. I treasured her so, yet I intentionally threw hard cubes of ice at her—violent in my attempts to find a safe space—as I escaped to my bedroom to shut out the world, Grammy included.

No one was safe. Once, when my Grandma (my Dad's Mum) was babysitting us, I wanted to take a 'get-well' card I'd made to my friend who lived down the street. Grandma did not want me out alone after sunset. But my six-year-old-self became angry, defied the wishes of a woman who had only my best interest at heart, headed outside, and slammed the door on her arm. The thin line of a scar that remained reminded me of an underline that could appear under the word anger. I wished it away so many times, and then avoided looking at it.

It was not out of character for me to vocally and assertively hold my ground, or tell people off.

Ongoing outbursts led Mum to arrange for me to see 'the talking doctor'. The way I understood it was I was to see 'that man' so that I could 'learn how to share again.'

And so I went to the talking doctor, but his efforts registered no effect. It was Uncle Bob, who reached me. He was my best pal, he told me stories about my Dad, and validated the special father-daughter relationship we'd had; the one that's reflected in all the family photos. Uncle Bob was one of the few people who could talk sense into me. He took me for lunches at places with paper placemats, and always let me order from the adult menu, then he dished out the real-deal in hard conversations.

Yes, I stopped letting people into my heart at the time the ink on the blue-prints for my future should have been nicely drying on the crisp sheet of a master architect's paper. And I continued my 'closed door to heart' policy through seven, eight…

CHAPTER 3

Semen Angustia
1992-2002

ANGUISH. THAT'S THE English equivalent. And, in the chaos of becoming father-less, I inhaled that seed of Anguish—a hybrid perennial produced for barren ground. Maybe the tiny seed had clung to the coattails of tragedy as disaster snaked in through the trailer's broken window and I'd swallowed it that very night my Dad had collapsed.

Like the Princess and the Pea, I constantly felt its presence, small as it was, its barbed edges catching the tender parts inside me as I moved about.

It germinated even as I lay still, for it contained a complete biological force—a fully detailed map of sorrow—all in its miniscule casing, intending to self-propagate with an inbuilt system of future.

All it needed was water, in the form of grief, to root, sprout, grow, bud, flower, and reproduce in burrs which latched on to, and proceeded to cover, every hint of promise and progress.

Innocence is fertile ground. The stem wound around my insides as a parasitic vine envelops a tree. Every breath I took nurtured the Anguish plant, encouraging sorrow to thrive. Thorns cut deep, and a tangle of leaves in my throat choked out my authentic voice.

I completed grade two and three, having turned eight in February, while at the same time, I saw myself as filling the role of Mum's best friend. I played the role of a woman, sipping coffee, across from her at the table, I believe—with my tomboy ways, I fit perfectly into the spot of the man at her side watching movies, I may have been relieved by filling an emptiness inside me to take on the part of the nanny-of-sorts, willingly protecting and carting around my younger siblings, but, most of all I was the child at her heels, clinging to the only parent I had left.

Then, all of a sudden, there was another man. He was going to be her husband. He stepped into a ready-made family, and I could not comprehend why. She had me.

Too young to process continuity, I viewed it as betrayal. The new arrangement took my child-mind to new levels of rage. I believed he could never take my Dad's place.

They married when I was eight. My sister and I were asked to call him Dad. My twin brothers, in post-toddlerhood, simply absorbed the situation.

I decided I didn't like him before they married. I simply believed he was a threat. I found everything he did intolerable. He entered the picture with good and honest intentions—but I had already established a choreographed dance of being bestie with my Mum. He was a reminder that I'd lost my Dad. It was, perhaps, that I wanted everyone to hurt as much as I did.

From this state of pain, I directed my attention to another man. An invisible, all powerful one: God. At eight, I was a child on a spiritual search. My concept of faith was already instilled through church attendance, and the necklace I'd been given: a rosary. The same one I'd held, moving my tiny fingers along its beads while in prayer during those days my father clung to life.

I flip-flopped between hope and anger. Beseeching God to tell me where my Dad was—in heaven?—and cursing the all-knowing presence for having taken my Dad away.

So eager was I to spiritually evolve, that I made it a quest to understand where my Father now resided. Was there such a thing as heaven? Would I ever see my Dad or my Brother again? What was the point of existence?

A girl of eight, totally engaged in a holy search, while entangled in with a vine named Anguish, with flowers called Fury; their scent manifesting as temper, unpredictability, name calling, and even bullying. Such contrast between a sacred quest and an explosive core.

As Fury's petals fell, they burned my insides and set off wildfires wherever they landed—mostly in the pit of my stomach. I shut down, to protect myself from the plant's toxicity; began building a hard shell to protect my heart.

In September 1992 I began grade three, followed the next year with grade four. But during that school year we moved house, which meant moving schools.

Rather than continue in grade four, it was decided that I'd go back to grade three. A new school meant new people, which took the sting out of reentering grade three among a student population I knew.

I moved through elementary school in a blur of dysfunction; simply existing. I continued to question the meaning of life. I filled the protective role of the eldest sibling, and carried on with the search for my soul.

In February 1997 I turned thirteen. Officially a teenager, and in grade seven, I auditioned, for a third time, for the Young Canadians, a performance group renowned for their presence within the Calgary Stampede. And the third time was a charm—so I thought. Yes, I made it.

I was buoyed by performing and dancing and making new friends in the group, but every minute of dance class made my previous worst moments a picnic. The dance instructor did nothing to boost my low self-esteem, routinely yelling at me in front of large groups.

Passionate and extroverted, I channeled my energy into causes—from protesting littering, to refusing to enter stores that supported child labour.

My 'gathering people together' skills were focused on not having people left out. My shadow side may have been overwhelming at times, stubborn too, but on the flip side was a girl who really longed to make a difference in the world; a girl with a huge heart and wildly optimistic picture of humanitarianism.

My spiritual search was one of constant questions. My version of God was always changing, and I was always curious, seeking new perspectives. Ultimately the search had to be about finding reason for the sudden loss of my Brother, and then my Father.

I never took the bible as hard fact, but I loved the mystery and the metaphorical lessons. I never doubted that Jesus walked the earth, nor that he was a powerful human with very deep and divine lessons, but I never bought into the idea of only one God, or one powerful teacher. I loved the teachings of many spiritual sects and religious viewpoints. I suppose the most important thing to me, for a long time, was simply to believe.

I wanted sun and joy all of the time. I had no respect for, or understanding of, the darkness.

For as long as I can remember I was driven deeply by masculine qualities: action, movement, direction, responsibility, strength, intellect, and accomplishment. I always had something to do and somewhere to go; forever searching for the finish line. The Kori that took on causes, right a wrong, without stopping to enjoy where I was in a moment, never pausing to feel the pain of a broken heart; just brute force, ploughing forward. It helped me control the parasitic vine that felt more at home in my body than I did.

In my times of rage, when I felt fearful or lacked control, I'd be the silverback gorilla, fighting to hold my stance. It was also not uncommon for me to puff out my chest through the use of language—loud. Grace was not present. I was powerless to soften into letting go of control; had to have the last word.

September 2000 signaled the new millennium, and the start of high school. I enrolled in a Catholic high school that offered a freedom via its unique delivery of curriculum. Students who required a flexible schedule or wanted more independence attended the academic school. My dance schedule required it, and I had the self-discipline to take on the non-traditional classroom style.

I thrived in this environment. No one told me what to do or how to do it. Three years of independent study to complete high school, with the added surprise of excelling in a few subjects. Though I'd never enjoyed writing, I received one-hundred percent on my final Social Studies essay, and I rocked biology.

Yet, even with this success, there was a dark side. In grade ten I began thinking about wanting to die—yes, as in taking my life. I may have thought about it before that, but high school is my first clear memory of actively thinking about not living. More than once I prayed to God to take me—prayed with the same might and passion as I had at six when I'd begged God to spare my Dad. But God hadn't spared my Dad, and God didn't take me. But the vine of Anguish flourished.

Instead of dying, I went into a prison of self-hate. Something clicked in my psyche and allowed unhealthy body image messages to hold me captive.

My dancer's body was a kind of claim to fame. I identified my worth with my physical anatomy, yet never felt pretty, even though others said I was. It didn't matter since I couldn't tell myself.

→‣◉ ◉‣←

All humans have a masculine and feminine form within. The key is to establish a balance—the yin yang. We will often have a more dominant force, and without conscious work, we can become out of balance.

When I look back, I understand how others could have been intimidated by my brand of me. Hell, if I overwhelmed me, it had to have had an effect on others.

It would be years before I could associate darkness and femininity in one concept. It would also be years of self-study into the inner workings of my soul before I could entertain the idea that femininity has strength.

Who knew that getting one-hundred percent on an essay, and acing biology, would connect me to reigniting with life, and directly link to my career?

But before I could fully step into the healing powers of food, with deep and divine respect, I had to trudge through the world of eating disorders, among other living hells on earth, in order to emerge knowledgeable enough to help myself, and wise enough to know how to help others.

CHAPTER 4

Promise and Unworthiness

2002-2006

I BECAME ADEPT at regulating the growth of the parasitic vine inside me. I found ways to cope—causes to champion. In this way, I basically started removing the buds before they bloomed into toxic flowers. I weeded vigilantly, but never quite got to digging out the roots—they were buried in a spot where it was difficult to find my footing, let alone sink a shovel. Instead, I pruned the plant when I could, and endured the anxiety when it sent out new shoots that tried to strangle me.

When grade twelve ended, a whole new level of life appeared. I asked myself, "Am I done? Am I an adult now?" Physically, I was the same person as I had been the day before graduation, but there was a liberating shift. Eager to shed that sandbox-dirty-knees playtime, I needed a peaceful transition to the future. But the past didn't fade. I couldn't drive away from it like I could from the school building, watching it disappear in the skewed rectangle of rearview mirror. The past was always in my peripheral vision.

After graduation, June 2002, I took a year off education to work, save money, and travel.

Waitressing at a local pub was incredible: fun, easy, and enjoyable. I picked up additional work as a receptionist, and I volunteered in the costume department for the Young Canadians.

Dedicated to a goal, I saved about $7000 and bought a car—a 1993 Honda Accord. I was proud of myself. Additional savings were labeled for a van so that I could travel across Canada during the next summer. I loved the idea of seeing the world, and I thought there was no better way to ignite adventure than to start by seeing the space beyond my own back yard.

During my year off I spent a lot of time thinking about what I wanted to do. Post-secondary education was a major deal in my family. In my heart I knew I was on this earth for something big, but had no idea what that something was.

I loved the idea of designing show costumes, so I applied to Olds College for fashion design. Nutrition was also highly intresting to me. Despite my distorted image, and issues that involved my own food intake, I understood the healing properties of food. I'd loved biology in high school.

In my free time, I spent time researching diabetes and creating a health plan for a family member. There was so much satisfaction in the science and helping that I became even more fascinated by food's powerful role in wellness. I discovered a course at the Southern Alberta Institute of Technology (SAIT) called Nutrition for Healthy Lifestyles, and I applied.

In 2003 I was accepted to SAIT. I was thrilled.

It also completely contrasted my concept of body hatred.

Perhaps the toxic environment of dance class—being told, on more than one occasion, that 'we' were gaining weight—combined with media images, had ingrained a distorted view of myself. I was affected by negative commentary—a male friend texted he hoped I didn't gain the 'freshman 15'—the obsession of being skinny was rooted in these messages.

The body-hate prison in my mind may have been set in high school, but there was seemingly no release date. It appeared to be a life sentence. And studying nutrition was the equivalent to being a chameleon; I disguised my issues by blending in with the healthy eating environment. It was also a lifeline, setting the stage for a future which couldn't come soon enough—and didn't.

Mum knew something was wrong, as Mum's do, but I became defensive when she brought up the subject of eating. Anger surfaced; I wasn't ready to face my truth. I counted calories like a maniac, averaging 900 a day. For those who are not aware of appropriate food intake:

Nine-hundred calories is not fucking enough to live on.

The scale was my master, its read-out my wheel-of-fortune. Numbers decided my fate for the day, therefore my mood. At 116 pounds all was fine with the world.

Not so at 125; cause to instantly morph into a self-loathing, foul-mouthed monster. The only escape was smoking weed while eating five-cent candies; paradise, albeit a temporary state of euphoria.

Eating disorders are messier than a baby in a highchair with his first dish of SpaghettiOs. They are more math-mindset than menu—kilograms, pounds (2.20462 pounds to the kilo), stones (14 pounds equals 1 stone), sizes on labels, ratings as in 'she's a ten'. Cognitively I recognized size 26 jeans were not an indication of being 'fat', but obsession does not appreciate intellect or reality.

I was judge, jury, and jailer. No one seemed to understand my reality. I worked out all the time, but for the wrong reasons. I spent too much time in front of the mirror cursing body parts; hated my nose, thought my forehead was big, wanted a boob job, felt I looked like a boy. My eyes saw the reflection of a tremendously overweight person not worthy enough to walk along the street, let alone grace the planet.

Had I not experienced this, I would never have believed a human brain capable of such misrepresentation.

I cleverly cut corners in my role as a slave to food. The kinds of things I did privately to starve myself did not reflect what I was learning, loving, and understanding in school. Toxic chemicals, in the form of artificial sweeteners, fertilized the vine of Anguish. Mood swings featured heavily in each day.

I remained a hostage for about four years, though there were times of clarity—some loosening of the chains, time off for 'good behaviour'—but I often managed to reoffend and end up back in solitary.

I was Kori the student who understood clean eating concepts and embraced the curriculum at SAIT; designed healthy eating plans for others, excelled through the course.

And I was Kori the inadequate, an unworthy piece of shit lurking under the layer of talent, pushing away her potential and intellect, allowing herself only to glimpse small portions of her accomplishments—like visiting hours to a prisoner on death row; like a small bowl of rice to a starving child—tidbits of recognition, where consistent accolades were clearly deserved.

And I understood that praise was merited. At SAIT I studied hard because I wholeheartedly adored what I was learning. I absolutely loved every part of school, and through that I was, thankfully, forced to recognize the amazing grades I received.

That little light, of mine, began to shine. I discovered how the power of self-love could transform a person's life; and that year—my twentieth on this planet—I dedicated my life's work to empowering humans to find self-love.

The extraordinary desire to make the world a better place was right up my alley. Big visions. It was the first time in my whole life I felt smart.

I graduated with honours.

It was a remarkable period and, while I battled the eating issues, I discovered author and motivator, Louise Hay. Her beliefs about healing illness matched those I'd always held. Illness is an expression of a thought pattern gone sideways. Our bodies are reflections of our thoughts and belief systems. It was liberating to read the work of a woman I deeply admired stating the concepts I'd formed long ago.

I began devouring all kinds of books, discovered many spiritual authors, and joined *A Course In Miracles* study group which my aunt hosted. Those deep conversations that I had longed for with others began happening. The world was my oyster.

The twisting vine inside me became dormant—resembling a shriveled Virginia Creeper clinging to a lattice on the side of a house in a Prairie winter. I began to breathe. And Louise Hay's words from *You Can Heal Your Life* became a permanent sticky on my inner-whiteboard. Hay specifically talks about the word 'NO'—stating, "by saying no to you, I am saying yes to me."

I began to comprehend the meaning of boundaries and the relationship to saying 'no'. To me, boundaries meant that I'd explored what I was not willing to tolerate in my life and what I was not willing to accommodate. By beginning to survey what I needed to thrive—and I had a lot of exploration to do—I understood it would eliminate that which had suffocated me.

That same year, my Grammy passed away; a pivotal moment in all of the lives of the humans she touched. A woman of sheer grace, she was a healer. Never one to be influenced by the pressures of society, her strong convictions and forward thinking placed her ahead of her time. I like to think she was a 'green witch' and that I inherited her 'nutritional-herbal-healing-potion-crafting' gene. Grammy was the first of her siblings to pass away. Her strength had always inspired us, and continued to as she chose to stay at my Aunt's house over a hospice, and allowed us to come and visit her whenever we wanted.

We each got to say our own versions of goodbye. I remember magical moments when we were all there—Aunts, Uncles, and Cousins—holding hands around her bed in a prayer circle. Belief, in all its forms, was a family value. When I was alone with her, I lay against her chest and we talked about heaven. I asked her where she thought she was going, and if she was scared. She told me she would send me an email if she was able to. I still check my inbox. Her presence is most often apparent when I'm crafting foods and potions, or studying them.

I began to embrace the power of thriving in life, and said goodbye to Grammy. The rest of my life waited. I made a decision to travel and work overseas. "Australia," I said. "Here I come." PS: "I'm bringing a bit of baggage."

⊷══ ══⊶

Self-Love is wholly dependent on our inner-thoughts which are programmed through a combination of our experiences and genetics. In what may be a surprise to some, worthiness is not dependent on the interlocking material and social aspects of our lives—bank account, job status, race, body composition, complexion. Worthiness is a consistent self-love. Self-love requires us to love the whole, all the parts of ourselves. Every fucking cell.

Anyway, I was a novice in worthiness. I didn't love every cell. I hated a few million of them. Though I had completed the theory work on worthiness, by reading books and being in study groups, I'd only just started my personal apprenticeship with true love.

I had no idea, then, that my future entailed a tragically wild ride. That I'd heal and experience goodness, then plunge into a living hell. If I'd known what was going to come after Australia, maybe I'd never have returned from down-under.

CHAPTER 5

All the Colours, Upside Down

2006-2011

ON NOVEMBER 06, 2006, at twenty-two years old, I left Calgary for a one-year adventure in Australia.

I had no idea how to navigate my way through an airport, let alone how to survive in another country, but on arrival my baggage seemed lighter.

Perhaps it was a flashback to child-imaginings of being upside down—the way we picture being in Australia based on the way globes look, and atlases denote the continent—even the way we refer to it as 'down under' has topsy-turvy written all over it. But something in my 'shake-things-up' gutsy decision allowed the eating issues and distorted body image to leave.

The twisty vine inside me didn't care for the outback's climate either. The shriveled stem of the creeper hung on my inner-frame without leaf or bud.

I'd flown into Cairns, and bought tickets for the "Oz Experience", a tour bus. Final destination: Brisbane.

But it was another place that found me and opened its arms in a warm welcome, held my hand, nurtured my fears, and rocked me to sleep at night.

Airlie Beach is home of the famous Whitehaven Beach and the Whitsunday Islands. A town of epic splendor.

I will never forget the first view of Airlie; approaching it by first driving up a hill, then experiencing the reveal from above; miles of azure waters that rivaled the colour of the sky. At the base of the hill was a picturesque harbor—I had never seen its equal. At first sight, every cell in my body wanted to learn to sail.

I booked a ticket, as a passenger, on a boat called Freight Train. It was a tour sailboat—monohull (that means one hull—some boats have more than one) that took passengers out on a three-day, two-night trip through parts of the Whitsundays (a seventy-four island area of exceptional natural beauty with Arlie at its hub). I'd never sailed before, but over that weekend I fell passionately in love with the vessels, the peace they represented, the challenges they invited.

Through sheer determination I landed a job on a trimaran named 'Avatar' on which I'd spend the next eight months as crewmember, a host—hostie in Australia—to passengers sailing through one of the most magical places on the planet. I worked, the only female crew, alongside Tristan, the skipper, and Ferg, the deckhand.

Getting used to the galley was a major triumph for me because I suffered incredible bouts of sea-sickness during the early days on the boat. It took quite a few trips before I adjusted. I was determined, and it was worth it.

Tristan, a keen chef, demonstrated a lot of patience and taught me so much about cooking. He was an amazing skipper, with a fantastic deckhand, Ferg; they taught me how to sail. My work uniform was a bathing suit, and my job description included touring the Whitsundays. I treasured every single moment: from each morning's spectacular sunrise, to sleeping soundly in a giant cradle called Avatar. In-between, we fed eagles, spotted whales and dolphins, and celebrated the sacredness of life.

"Well the sun rose. With so many colors it nearly broke my heart.
It worked me over like a work of art. And I was a part of all that."

Artist: Dar Williams, Lyrics: After All

We caught crabs for dinner. Conversations filled in the empty spaces and curious corners inside each of us. Collectively we grew. Independently I learned. Sunny days, starry nights, the wet times, the sunny-hot-dry spells, and the cyclone season—we sailed through them all. So deep in love was I with the lifestyle, I wanted to live on a boat forever.

My job was to cook for twenty to thirty-five passengers, make beds, and generally cater to the guests. At the time I was hired I had no idea how to cook, and had a severe aversion to touching raw meat. The second night's dinner was roast—with Tristan's help, I managed the challenge—one of many. Yes, I let the I-can't-touch-raw-meat feeling go and made a full dinner.

I also fell head-over-heels in love with a man in Australia; one of the best humans ever. A gypsy and free spirit with wild dreadlocks, he worked as a sailor. When I met him on 'Freight Train' he owned only a surfboard, a couple of pairs of 'boardies' (shorts for surfing), and a van in which he lived.

My Aussie sailor showed me how to have fun. He taught me to eat ice-cream without obsessing about my body image; supplemented my sailing lessons; encouraged me to drink rum and dance until five in the morning. He demonstrated full hearted and whole-souled living and invited me to experience all the glory of life.

He was at home on the sea—a dolphin or pirate in a past life; perhaps both. He knew the coast, weather patterns, and boats intimately. An incredible swimmer, nothing brought that man more joy than sailing and, of course, imparting that knowledge with the humans he loved; generously, in my case.

I learned to sail. I learned to trust. I learned to accept love.

Australia was my chapter to learn fun and also to learn to never say 'never'. I loved every moment.

I turned twenty-three in Australia. Happy Birthday, Kori. Kori Reborn.

As our relationship progressed, and more time passed, I returned with my Aussie sailor to Canada. We hoped we could live in landlocked Alberta. But he belonged to the sea. In total, we'd attempt to be together for five years. There were different plans for us. Heart wrenching as our goodbye was, we each knew we needed to pursue our individual callings.

In 2009, when I was twenty-five, I returned to Australia. And I turned twenty-six in New Zealand. That chapter of my life was equivalent in phenomenality to my first year in Australia.

New Zealand offered absolute joy. Perhaps I was stepping into myself—having had the Australian experience. A more stable Kori simply allowed herself to drink in every drop of the elixir that is New Zealand.

The unique culture embraced me, its people so genuine and warm. The geography begged connection with every footstep in every place. I lived in a beach town called Mount Maunganui. I spent my days working at 'Jenny Craig' and my nights hanging out on the Beach or running the Mount.

It was at the Mount that I ran my first ten-kilometre race. The Mount allowed me to sample the excitement of simply being alive and celebrate the joy of physical movement.

My heart attached itself to New Zealand. It told my brain that I would leave a piece of myself there. And that was okay because I knew a part of my spirit would join that of all who have been enchanted by the country.

Returning to Canada brought with it the difficult task of adjustment.

It was a bumpy re-entry; I ached for Australia and New Zealand. In December, at the Jenny Craig Christmas party, the owner explained to me that all the locations in New Zealand and Australia had been sold. I would not be returning.

I did not have a visa, and my connection to a solid company there was affected by the sale.

I'd worked at Jenny Craig in Canada, after SAIT, then for a time in Australia, and in New Zealand, consulting with clients one-on-one. I'd loved helping, and people trusted me with their deepest darkest secrets. I'd felt honored. After I returned to Canada, I was still with Jenny Craig, but as a program director, selling Jenny's program. But in my new role, working within a demographic that did not comprise wealthy clients, felt unethical; I wasn't comfortable selling to those who could not afford it.

More than anything else, I wanted to move back to New Zealand and reunite with contentment and joy.

My Aussie sailor chapter was over. I hurt. I was angry with love. I was even mad at him. I despised life. I was furious with God's stupid plan. Life had deceived me again. My secure lifestyle 'down-under' was essentially buried.

I came undone. And, in the way patterns replicate on a stuck keyboard, and the way lessons are repeated until they are learned, I became cold and distant.

I so wanted to 'get' life. And I worked hard to do it. I focused on the positive. By February, having recently turned 27, I was living in the coolest sixteenth-floor condo, right downtown, with my friend, Emily. We filled our days with tea-time and heart-to-heart conversations. She and I spent nights drinking wine and dancing at a gay bar next to our apartment. Sunday afternoons slipped by watching movies and eating Indian food.

But, there was a darker energy stored in the roots of that withered vine. Its sap crept up into the deadwood like a venomous snake rising and slinking through a tunnel. My discontent fed the vine, fertilized it with mistrust; the plant set about its own lifecycle, preparing the toxic flowers from hell for the longest blooming season ever known.

I remember lying in the bathtub, yelling at God, and severing my relationship with spirit.

→▬◉ ◉▬←

We should all spend more time appreciating our best-friend relationships. I have been lucky enough to live with besties, and each was an amazing chapter of sisterhood, connection, self-exploration and growth.

"We are all walking each other home."

Modern philosopher, Ram Dass

But there were more lessons before I could consistently enjoy the delicious fruits of friendship. It was a shock to discover that I was still learning to walk, given I'd soared, sailed, and sprinted down-under. Coming home to a geographical place was a major adjustment. Finding my home inside myself was even more difficult.

Living a life according to my values, and earnestly finding the way to my heart and soul was a daily challenge for me. I believe I'd lost my ability to create and uphold boundaries at a very young age. And so I basically arrived back in Canada and took the first connection to the deepest, darkest, dankest place ever, where the seeds of the vine of Anguish are planted.

A nightmarish descent to hell on earth; slow, plodding steps, wading into the swamp—downhill, deeper, steeper—until my mud-caked feet could not move, and the gravity of darkness pulled me in a slow-motion plummet.

Chapter 6

Contrast

2011

WITH MY BODY, mind, and soul plunged into the depths of a bleak Alberta winter—such a contrast from New Zealand—the roots of the twisty vine inside me found strength in permafrost. Thrilled to be 'home', the vine invited everything cold, callus, and abusive to nourish its growth.

All I wanted was a fresh re-start with love and joy.

Sixteen days after I'd turned twenty-seven years old, I quit working in a position in which, ethically, I couldn't reconcile.

Sixteen days after I'd turned twenty-seven years old I envisioned helping others and teaching bootcamps full-time.

Sixteen days after I'd turned twenty-seven years old I'd already risen to a girlfriend's suggestion that I meet someone. He and I had exchanged a series of short text messages.

Sixteen days after I'd turned twenty-seven years old, a girlfriend came over and helped me pick an outfit. I was looking forward to being taken out on a date; excited to be indulged a little.

Sixteen days after I'd turned twenty-seven years old, missing my Aussie sailor, I decided 'Prince Charming on his white horse' would arrive to save me.

My girlfriend was still with me when 'he' arrived.

He showed up at the condo with wine and a case of beer. He sat on the couch, and didn't say a word, at first. I couldn't seem to hold a conversation either. I wasn't myself. My girlfriend stayed.

When I did speak, I couldn't express myself as I usually did.

Something felt off when he finally spoke.

His tone was alarming; my gut called it disrespectful, but my mind ate it up. I decided I appreciated his forwardness with me and loved how he could stand up to me.

Yes, I liked that he put me down.

Sixteen days after I turned twenty-seven years old, I shelved positivity and encouraged the fucking vine to establish itself much like Jack's beanstalk—fast, furious, thick, mammoth.

When my roommate-bestie came home that night, she saw three totally wasted people on the sofa. She told me later that the place reeked of alcohol, the vibe was all wrong, and she'd felt thoroughly uncomfortable.

She instantly saw all the red-flags that I'd mistaken for variations of fleece blankets.

And it wasn't over. He drove me to a restaurant for dinner—no, I don't remember where; yes, that's bizarre for a first date; appalling that he was in no shape to drive; unbelievable I'd participate; but this wasn't a happy fairy tale, even though I was under some kind of spell. We went to a nightclub after we ate; no waiting in line—he knew the bouncers.

We sat at the bar and drank a lot of grape vodka-and-water. I didn't pay for anything. I'd never done anything like this before. It was a thrill. We cabbed back to his place. I woke up in the morning wearing his shirt and nothing else.

I walked home. He went to pick up his car which had been towed because he parked it in the middle of the road. I thought it was funny and named us 'the shit show'.

Red flags? I was emotionally colour blind.

Warning sirens? I was essentially deaf.

Speaking my truth? I might as well have been completely mute.

My intuition was screaming at me from the first moment, and I doused my instincts with poison, and the toxic petals set it alight.

He called to ask me out the next night. I had to ask him what vehicle he drove; I know, it's crazy that I had zero recall.

Our second date took place at a coffee shop—I drank tea.

At one point another man walked in and I looked up in the kind of way one does when someone enters a coffee shop—ring-a-ling, door opens, look up in coffee shop casual acknowledgement. Prince Not-Charming immediately accused me of checking the guy out. As I shrugged off the accusation, my gut sent me a message: *Not. Appropriate. Behaviour.*

I told my intuition that he was just being a guy. My gut sent me another message: *I'm not talking about 'his' behaviour, I'm letting you know yours is unacceptable.*

And in the way one throws another log on the fire, I watched another toxic petal fall and singe my value system; after all, the vine was in the perfect environment and had an excess of blossoms.

When my Aussie sailor was so kind to me, it had felt foreign and uncomfortable, but it had been quite fantastic too. This new guy was offensive in the way he 'stood up to me'—in other words, treated me like shit—and, bizarrely, it felt like home.

It felt like the home I deserved.

It appealed to my senses as would freshly baked cookies, flannel sheets in winter, or a nightlight in a dark hallway.

How fucked up is that?

That night, after the coffee shop, we drove to his place and watched a movie. Within hours of shrugging off the accusations he'd made about me checking out another guy, I told him about my dreams to own a retreat center, one where I would empower women. I shared with him how I'd wanted to do this for a long time, and how I'd made a vision board to illustrate my dream.

⇢▸═◁ ◁═▸◁⇠

I confided my desires to have a retreat center, a place for the empowerment of women, to a man who was treating me with disrespect. Oh, the irony.

A white horse carrying Prince Charming? The 'C' was missing.

The vine inside me was instantly attracted to his abusive personality—had essentially found the perfect gardener and maintenance man. It shot a cluster of leaves around my seeing heart and dropped fiery petals on my self-esteem. It was as if a library of sacred books had been intentionally burned down, and an ugly thicket had grown quickly through its ruins.

pH—ironically, Prince Charming without the C—stands for 'potential of Hydrogen', is represented on a scale of 1 to 14, with 7 as a neutral point. A value below 7 indicates acidity, and the lower the number the stronger the acidity. A value over 7 indicates alkalinity. Alkalinity is the name given to a solution to neutralize acid. The pH value is profoundly important to all life-systems. Each organism requires an optimal, specific pH level in which to thrive.

Potential of Hydrogen or Prince Harming. I'd always loved biology. Also, word-play.

I began a pattern of betrayal, engaged in an infidelity to my own truth, became disloyal to my friends, and deeply hurt my first true love—my Aussie sailor.

This dangerous world brought out the absolute worst in me. I would become emotionally numb, defensive, volatile, and violent. In my sick mind, at the time, 'too much to drink' was a valid excuse. I can see now the insanity of this, but I could not comprehend it at the time.

It was as if we were on a stage and life was no longer real. The first date was the first act of a tragedy. It would be the first of many acts containing hundreds of scenes in a long-running hit.

The parasitic vine in me loved acidity. Prince Charming without the C—PH—fed it. The vine consumed me; nearly killed me. And sometimes I wanted it to.

Writing this is borderline embarrassing, but this is a story of shining a light on shame.

CHAPTER 7

My Relationship with PH
2011

WE BECAME A couple.

He went away on a 'trip for the guys', and in the middle of the night I began receiving irrational text messages accusing me of cheating on him with my former boyfriend, the Australian sailor.

He claimed he saw me kissing him. Of course, this was impossible: my 'ex' was on another continent on the other side of the world. Though it was alarming, even frightening, to read these messages, I immediately went on the defensive to disprove his allegations. And after that, I decided, since his statements were beyond irrational, that he must have had too much to drink. There was no way he could have been serious.

The rollercoaster ride continued. This man had as many imbalances as I had, and he, too, exhibited the shadow side of all qualities. I surmised the difference was that his personality was narcissistic-psychopath, incapable of feeling true human emotions like compassion and authentic empathy, and I, on the other hand, dangerous as my behaviour was, had a functioning, emotional heart.

The combination of us was hazardous. Sometimes I walked on eggshells on top of eggshells; his drunken instability pushed us over the border to insanity. Other times it was cuddles and glorious partnership. The relationship could change as fast as flipping a light switch; zero to one-hundred in three seconds— from smile to inane fighting. Though we travelled together, spending lots of weekends in the mountains, or headed out to fantastic restaurants, we illustrated a huge disconnect. We both spoke similar stories of the lives we wanted to live, but we couldn't walk the talk for long.

28

The rest of 2011 was a reckless and tenuous time of building a bad relationship on a pitiful foundation. Refusing to be conscious of the issues, I believed in making 'fucked-up love' work. So sure was I that I had to make this relationship a success that I chose to put a lot of unhealthy 'stuff' into the category of normal. I forgot myself, placed PH on a pedestal, and undertook a ritual of worshipping him.

I admired him despite the fact he lied to me; I was lying to myself anyway, so we were two dishonest people. I looked up to his strength and popularity when my gut told me there were other women in the picture. I revered him, even celebrated him, viewing him as my leader, of sorts—believing that being in his kingdom was enough; I had no right to access any of his secrets; I did not require transparency from him. I put his appetite for alcohol down to his manliness; same for his appeal for porn.

He wanted me; therefore I was fortunate for being wanted. I was grateful to have been 'chosen', which meant I didn't need to question his erratic behaviour which included his cruel treatment of me.

I questioned my sanity and clung to the concept that he was somehow my saviour. And I learned how to treat him with the equivalent of his brand of abuse; mine manifested in an extreme level of neediness.

The extent of his power surges and rages included regular freak-outs about my alliance or loyalty to my Aussie ex. My sailor and I had been together for five years; it was unreasonable to think that someone would just forget another human who was part her heart.

Irrational as it was, he intended me to erase the memory of my former boyfriend, and get rid of any physical evidence that the relationship existed. Delete my Aussie sailor from my history? According to the Prince's royal decree: yes. And so, in an 'or course, your highness, consider it done', I carried out the order.

Against all inner-guidance, one particularly 'dark' night, after he'd lost it on me again for having evidence on Facebook of my relationship in Australia, I went online and deleted every album of Down-Under. All those illustrations of fond memories wiped out—gone. I went a step further. I found my Aussie sailor online and blocked him from contacting me. It wasn't far enough. I blocked every member of his family, too.

My heart broke. I knew it would hurt my sailor, but I succumbed to the dysfunction. This was the beginning of losing touch with those I cared for; the start of total isolation.

These demands to delete people from my life happened within the first week of knowing him. Yes, how powerful is that? I totally questioned my own sanity, my voice, my truth. Instant irrational responses to a man I'd just met.

I recall making a scrapbook for my brother. It was an album of memories from our trip to Burning Man. I had a picture of a group—about twenty people, one of which was my Aussie ex—I didn't mean to leave it in plain view, but it was there and 'he', the monster-who-shall-not-be-named-but-only-referred-to-as-'PH', saw it.

What followed was accusation after accusation of my still being in love with the sailor. It was insane. I had already deleted all pictures of my previous life and all important memories to me from my computer; I had blocked my sailor and all those with whom my sailor was associated, and yet one person in a group of twenty in a photo scrapbook for my Brother set PH off.

It enraged me. I lost control. I fucking snapped.

I directed the anger toward the scrapbook, tearing it apart in a fit of rage. Screaming, crying, trying to breathe. I'd never before seen this side of myself; it frightened me, but mostly I felt humiliated, so I pretended it didn't happen.

When I was able to gather myself, I saw what I'd done. The hurt ran deep. I'd destroyed a piece of art I'd devoted to making for someone I loved. I cried some more. I saved the torn copy. I gave the broken book to my Brother a few years later—couldn't bring myself to fix it.

--=◦ ◦=--

Why the hell didn't I see what was going on? Why didn't I walk away? Why was I ignoring the voices screaming in my head that something was not right? I don't know.

Fool me once, shame on you. Fool me twice (or for 2 more years over and over and over) shame on me.

There were so many reprehensible examples. There were myriad dangerous situations involving 'him', PH. But this is not a book about shaming anyone. This is the story of me, shared so that I can help others. It is a book about healing. It is not a book about hate. It is a book about love.

CHAPTER 8

Normalizing Abnormal
2011-2012

IRONICALLY, *THE YEAR of Living Dangerously* is an Australian film, a romantic war drama, produced from a book by the same name. In my case, in a remake, I'd need to change the title: Multiple Years of Living Absofuckinglutely Dangerously. I'd place it in the genre of horror. My movie trailer would encapsulate a random journal entry, such as this:

> Over the past few months he's had a few VERY angry drinking episodes where he's freaked out at me, calling me a dirty whore, the worst fuck he has ever had, and… he even sent me pictures of other women he's been dating. One of them is his house cleaner; says he was involved with her since the day after we broke up. He claims it was nothing. But it seems rather odd to me.
>
> I don't know what it is that I'm holding onto. I BEG him to love me when he's angry. It's a crazy attachment of energy. I don't know how to walk away, and, right now, I don't know how to stay. I cry every day.
>
> EVERY. SINGLE. TORTUOUS. DAY.
>
> Why can't it just FINISH?
>
> I say that I believe I love him. My family and friends STRONGLY disagree with this. My dear friend, Kim, even said that I don't speak to him lovingly, and my body language does not show love. She says I'm guarded all the time.
>
> I am guarded.
>
> I walk on eggshells.

I never have any idea what his mood will be. I'm fearful when he goes drinking with his friends. I'm scared to make other plans. I'm afraid that if things do not go one-hundred percent HIS WAY, then he will just leave me, or hurt me, or harass me.

I have tried to walk. He keeps coming to get me. Or, I run back to him.

Somewhere I have crossed this up with losing my Dad. I don't know how it's become enmeshed. I don't even know what 'crossed this up' means.

I lie, compromising ALL relationships in my life for the one with him. And I don't think he gives a rat's ass. I care more about him than I do about me.

I want to die. I wish I was not on this planet. I feel like the biggest loser ever to live—EVER. I don't know how to fix this all at this point.

⇥▰◉ ◉▰⇤

This typifies the conditions in which I existed from the day I met PH in 2011. The year played out in a series of surreal dramas. Nothing was as it had been in the past, and it appeared to me that the future was a motivational calendar for everyone else but me. Basically I was tomorrow-less; all my time seemed to be the same tragedy playing on a continuous loop.

One thread that connected me to any semblance of life was keeping a journal, albeit the entries did not begin with 'happy dear diary'. Erratic writing on a regular schedule. Recording the hate. Documenting and dating the dark deeds. Writing my weaknesses in order to be strong enough to survive. That's how I 'did' my time. That's how I 'only just' kept the poisonous vine inside me from choking the life out of me.

To look back and see that this period was not a 'phase' of a few months is shocking. To view the length of time I remained in a kind of darkness—the blackest kind that one fears, versus the blackest kind one knows and loves by smell, touch, hearing, and loving intuition— speaks to extreme dysfunction, the strength of spirit within such toxicity, and the tenacity of the human condition.

CHAPTER 9

Punish Me(nt)

2012

**"Similarly, adults often remain endlessly in
unhappy, abusive, or depriving relationships
by blaming their suffering on their own shortcomings,
their not having 'gotten it right' yet:
'If I can just get it right, the punishing
other will smile upon me.'
Such an interpretive pattern can keep someone
futilely trying to get it right forever."**

Clinical Psychologist, Author: Dr. Robert Stolorow

THE MORE I tried to 'get it right' the larger PH grew and the smaller I became.

In the universal habit of beginning a new year with a clean slate—a fresh page, white as snow, pretending bad stuff hadn't happened—I looked forward to restarting, and hoped for an epiphany. There were things I loved and knew I excelled at, and professional desires were surfacing. Then there was the relationship with him, one which dominated everything else. What well-adjusted people call 'nice, regular, enjoyable real life moments' were sparsely scattered among an abusive and dysfunctional daily routine.

January evidenced some promise. Though, career-wise, I felt lost, I knew I wanted to have a business, but wasn't sure how to make it a reality. When PH seemed supportive of my career path, we worked together as a team. He agreed I should quit my job at retailer Lululemon. He was in favour of my registering for courses to promote my dream. I began recertification in canfitpro, and started working on becoming certified with the Alberta Fitness Leadership Certification Association (AFLCA).

I ran a lot. Running provided freedom, and running with my friend, Laura, was sacred time. I hosted indoor Bootcamps, and reaffirmed how much I loved helping others. I called the Bootcamps my baby. My confidence grew. But in February I injured my foot. Though I could barely walk for a few months, I still did the AFLCA courses at Heavens Fitness. The staff gave me incredibly positive feedback and asked if I'd like to teach cycling classes.

My twenty-eighth birthday came and went—February 12. Birthdays are a big deal to me. PH did nothing to recognize it. It seemed we could never maintain the momentum of healthy couple-ship. In essence we had never attained or established it.

Hurt as I was, I rallied and we continued with a planned—unrelated to my birthday—getaway to Costa Rica. The day before the trip, we went to a pub. After he'd had too many beers, PH told me I was a useless, dependent person— 'useless and un-independent' was his actual slur. I left; he stumbled home much later. The next day, I engaged my amazing super-power to forget the negative words he'd spoken.

After our return from Costa Rica, I began integrating my work into Heavens Fitness, and began teaching at Peloton—I went there 'for' a cycling class and the owner said I was an amazing 'spinner', then asked if I'd like to work there; even asked me to do presentations on nutrition. The promise of Spring was already springing, and the positives poured in from outside sources. With prospects at Heavens, the City of Calgary, and the Jewish Centre—plus Bootcamp—I experienced a sense of achievement, and a view of a successful future. Though there was no money coming in at the time, hope was beginning to bud. I began a program called Move. Eat. Hug, with 'Andrea', a wellness professional whom I admired. I loved talking to her; she knew me inside and out. I developed so much trust and respect for her.

And, like most of the people in my life, she did not care for PH.

And yet, Kori the successful, future entrepreneur was eclipsed by, Kori, the submissive, self-doubting partner to him.

For PH's March birthday, I decorated the house in candles and balloons and we made a lobster dinner. I cried when I put the lobster in the boiling water.

I arranged for us to go dog sledding, since he'd never done that. He seemed to enjoy it. In addition to the lobster meal, we also had dinner reservations at Bonterra, but we decided to stay in and watch movies. It appeared that we almost-sometimes glimpsed the idyllic.

But as always, we cratered. The promise of spring dissipated—the darkness of a million cold winter's nights surrounded me, and once again the vine of Anguish thrived on his negative contributions. He threw 'everything he'd done for me' at me, stating that I "offered nothing to our relationship".

We were not a team, and he was not onside with my career plans and dreams.

More uncertainty and untruths pervaded. I knew he had a son—with whom he was not involved. But suddenly I became aware that, from day one with me, he'd regularly—usually daily—texted or communicated in other ways with the mother of his son. He'd kept this a secret; lied about it.

Though his son's mother seemed nice, I took a stand on having been lied to. I packed my suitcases and moved me and my dog, Merlot, back to my parents' house.

Home again, I told myself I'd finally had enough of his abuse. But… the thing is… well…

It's just that we'd already booked a trip to San Francisco.

I didn't know if I should go.

I went.

We talked about what we needed to do when we got back home to fix 'team us' We spoke of coming up with goals 'together', and getting couples' counselling; he finally agreed that we needed help.

In May, back with PH, I kept myself busy teaching cycling, Bootcamps, doing lunch-n-learns for Peloton and ING. I felt hopeful, yet deeply lonely.

There is a subconscious way of taking violence as a way of expression,
as a normality,

Actor, Activist: Salma Hayek

At the end of the month, my friend, Kim, reached a ten year anniversary with her firm. A group of us, including PH, headed to a local pub to celebrate, and drank to excess. We went back to Kim's for more drinks. And then he was gone. He'd left her place at some point. When we realized PH was missing, Kim and Laura returned home with me to check if he was there.

And the night exploded.

Kim and Laura watched it unfold; a buildup of hateful words, negative emotions, and repressed anger.

Anger shot out from him; not unusual after an alcoholic overindulgence. Rage bubbled inside me; I'd been drinking too. I threw a bottle of balsamic vinegar, and I pitched the three framed pictures of 'us and our dog' across the room. They shattered on the granite floor. I ripped a lamp out of the wall and hurled it at him.

There was broken glass everywhere. He reacted violently: physically and vocally.

I tore his shirt and threw myself against him, yelling, "YOU DO LOVE ME. I KNOW you do NOT think I am WORTHLESS."

PH repeated what he'd said to me in the past: that I was crazy and he did not love me.

My blood boiled; he did love me. I told ME that every day, only to be reminded most nights, by him, that he did not.

He pinned me down, his body weight on my face, and wrapped my hair around his hand, then knelt on my head. He was much bigger than me. Kim and Laura shoved him off me. And there I was, yelling, losing my mind, my heart, my soul. I sobbed relentlessly, madly trying to convince him that he did love me.

When the storm calmed some, and Laura and Kim had packed my bags and made me commit to leaving, I walked away with finger marks on my neck, blood on my skin, and bruising to my body.

His parting words: "You hit me first."

I love my girlfriends for what they did that night, and for the unconditional love and support they would display during my treacherous journey. I love them because they worked so hard to help me see. But, they could not reach the Anguish that caused my emotional blindness.

This episode of 'leaving him' would not be the last time. I would wind up forgiving the chaos and go back to him again and again.

Chapter 10

Grace and Her Evil Sister, Neglect

2012

I MOVED IN with Kim.

I presented as a person needing an enormous amount of understanding and care. Kim rose to the occasion with grace and tolerance. She began to teach me about unconditional love by loving me unconditionally.

I'd wake up each morning and wish I hadn't. I'd look at my tattoo, 'love wins', and want to cut it off me. Full-on panic attacks were frequent. Long runs allowed the pain from my injured foot to distract me from the agony in my heart. Most of the calories I consumed were from wine.

I called the women's shelter for help, but didn't follow through on the appointment; embarrassed, I couldn't bring myself to admit that I was in an abusive relationship.

Kim completely embraced the whole limitless love for Kori concept; I didn't even have two pennies to rub together. She nurtured me. But the tendrils of the vine were protected by some kind of impenetrable sap which prevented Kim's love from reaching the source of my pain. Her love was like care packages intended for a victim of misfortune, only to be intercepted by a corrupt imposter who wrote, in permanent marker, 'no such person!' over the address label.

Between wanting to die, and feeling dead, I cried a lot. Couldn't make it through an hour without tears; didn't matter who was around.

And then PH texted me.

Again.

And again.

He'd express his love for me in one text, then announce he was angry with me in the next. It was hard to keep up with him; I felt like a casualty just dragged in from a battlefield.

Seized by the need to take action, I decided to speak with PH's Mother, and contact his son's Mother. Both women validated PH's long pattern of abusive behaviour. They each confided shocking information. So powerful was my resolve to put closure on it all that I confronted PH with a 'you shouldn't be mad at me because you've been abusing me and lying'.

Then, in a rapid turnaround, he was deeply and profoundly sorry; convincingly so.

I waded further into the swamp. The vine sprouted more fast-growing branches that obscured the accounts of two women who knew him well, who'd shared clear evidence of his sick cruelty.

He apologized so many times. Heartfelt atonements delivered with such intense eloquence that I was rendered breathless.

I told myself, NO, those things the others said could not have happened. I set about mastering selective memories.

…deeply and profoundly sorry.

I believed him.

Kori, Kori, you're a sad, sad story,
So, how does your garden grow?
With a poisonous vine,
Nourished by wine,
And pretty lies all in a row.

⋅⊶⋅

One-hundred percent engaged, I was addicted to the drama of us. He put me down so low, and yet he was the only one that I felt could pick me up.

It is what I imagine heroin dependency is like.

On June 18th, 2012—three weeks after the violent breakup—I wrote 'Relationship Boundaries' on a page in my journal. Then I drew a large circle. Inside the circle I wrote words to represent what I wanted in a relationship. Outside the circle I penned practices and behaviours I would not tolerate.

Protected in the sphere were gem-like words: respect, love, family values, romance, connection, communication, health, growth, progression.

Beyond the unbroken curved line I penned the words: **name calling, physical abuse, addiction, feeling unworthy, emotional abuse, drugs, steroids, cheating.**

The inner circle was filled with descriptives of what many people have in their lives; what I wanted in my life. But, sadly, what was printed outside of the circle was my 'every day'.

Inside the seemingly impenetrable circle was what I desired. At that time, simply a pipedream.

It remains the saddest circle I've ever seen.

Never ever would I have pegged myself for a relationship so drastically unhealthy. And yet, there I was, unable to get the hell out.

Perhaps there was a sacred contract between the PH and me. One designed so that my freefall plunged me into an abyss far beyond the limits of self-hatred. I landed in 'vine' territory, where Anguish thrived. And I sat in the swamp of self-loathing, in what I believe was a design, intentionally orchestrated, which brought me to understand choice: grow or die.

Somewhere along the way, I'd handed all my power over to another human, one whom I idolized. One for whom I was willing to abandon all sense of self-worth; one whose 'love' required me to surrender my soul.

It would have been less painful to have sold it to the devil.

Chapter 11

Journaling to Live
2012

June 18, 2012

I'm really struggling. It's been three weeks since we broke up and I can't stop thinking about him. I'm in total denial about his lifestyle and about how he treats me. In some delusional way I feel he will change. He says he loves me, and he authentically cries when he sees me, yet in the past three weeks he has not only done NOTHING to fix this; he has continued to drink and freak out at me. I have found out some bad things about him from two significant people in his life: I am not the first girl he has hit; he has huge anger issues; his parents pay his child support… the list goes on. It's scary because I have my own experience with him verbally abusing me and hitting me. I still want him?!?!

Maybe he's a good person and that's what I see. Or maybe I am in actual denial. I'm completely detached from the pain and the actions that caused the pain.

This way of living is killing me. I'm in survival mode. I have not been able to breathe at times. I'm 119 pounds, have depressed and suicidal thoughts, and am out of energy, focus, drive, and will.

⇥▱ ▱⇤

July 2012 (no day was recorded)

What I see, believe, and want in a real loving relationship:

Two whole, self-loving individuals who make each other's lives more fulfilling. We'll talk for hours and feel like no time has passed. We'll share similar views, goals, and beliefs. We'll not always agree, but both feel heard, valued, and understood. We'll make dinner together, do home projects, travel, work out, and work toward our goals as a team. In this 'what I see, believe, and want in love' concept, my ideal partner will be my biggest fan.

He'll value and respect me.

He'll show love and affection.

He will know how to say sorry.

He will work at making me feel special, valued, and appreciated.

He'll love my friends and family, and know that my/our time with them is important.

He'll cherish me, and, when I am with that ideal partner, I will always know in my heart that if life fell apart he will be my rock.

He'll challenge me, hold his ground, and we will grow from our fights.

We'll work hard at communication.

I will trust him.

He will be open and never keep secrets.

He'll never be jealous. He'll trust my love for him.

We will take care of one another and not take each other for granted.

We may not always agree or see the same side, and we will fight, but we will always know that our love is solid.

We will give each other space and freedom, which will be easy to do because of the unshakable trust between us.

We can be our best and our worst around one another; we will explore what it is like to be human. We'll grow, evolve, become better— more loving, more forgiving.

We'll share a deep love, trust, and connection.

We'll freely express our feelings and experiences.

We'll be curious about one another, and ask questions.

We'll deeply care about everything, from secrets, fears, and goals to how each other's day unfolded, and what each other's favourite song is.

It doesn't mean it won't be hard at times—sometimes really hard. He will hold me, he will have great strength. He will look past my eyes and into my soul.

Two entries: mid-June 2012, the other within weeks—in July 2012. Oh, the extremes. The reality, and the hope. The first amplified such inner suffering. And the second, well, it magnified my despair and anchored me in hope.

The thing is, there's an edge of mistrust in the extremely repetitive and massively extensive list of the ideal qualities I wanted in a partner and for relationship. I now read so much fear into the 'ideal list'. "…hard times—sometimes really hard." "We will fight."

Fight? Apparently, that's what I thought people did in regular relationships.

Question to self: Why, in a list of 'what I want' would 'fight' not be replaced with 'healthy dialogue'?

Answer: The phrase 'healthy dialogue' wasn't in my consciousness at that time.

When I look back, I recognize many of these attributes are those which 'everyone' would like in a relationship. However, most of those qualities were components that I desperately needed in a relationship with myself.

But I would not meet myself for a while.

I had a lot more learning to do.

If I was going to work with others, help others heal, and support others through their journeys, then I first had to serve an apprenticeship of sorrow in order to get my journeywoman status.

CHAPTER 12

Security, Blankets, and Bullshit

2012

I CONTINUED TO live with Kim. She continued to love me unconditionally. PH and I continued to text. He said he wanted to make things work. The promises arrived one message after another: it can work.

And, he carried on drinking; lots of alcohol-induced reviews of me—horrible messages.

I decided to go out on a date with a guy. We went to celebrate the Calgary Stampede and 'PH' somehow happened to be walking by and saw me with the 'guy'.

Every July, hundreds of thousands of people visit the Calgary Stampede grounds and venues around the city over a ten day period. Crowds enjoy the fairground, afternoon rodeos take place in front of hundreds of spectators in the stadium, evening chuck wagon races followed by performances headlined by The Young Canadians—of which I'd been a member—entertain thousands. More people bustle about viewing western-themed art in a massive pavilion. Sellers demonstrating the latest food choppers, absorbent mops, and a gazillion other gadgets fill another huge indoor space.

The city comes alive with hundreds of 'hot spots' around town.

And, PH 'just happened' to see me with the guy I went on a date with?

We'd been split for seven weeks and he'd done nothing to fight for me, but apparently he felt I was still his property. He was angry. He gave me new names. Whore. Dirt Bag. Dirty Bitch. His messaging was relentless.

And all I wanted to do was make sure he wasn't mad at me.

One morning, as I was getting into my car and heading to meet someone from HR to sign papers at a meeting related to my new job, he called me. He sounded angry. Big surprise.

We'd previously had a 'perfectly good' weekend together—yes, I was still seeing him—but on this morning he told me that I deserved to hurt as much as he did and that he would ensure that happened.

Then he told me that he was going to go to Kim and tell her everything; that I'd been seeing him, and that by doing so she would never want to be my friend again. He promised me that she would kick me out and I would have nowhere to live.

Panic mode struck. I knew he would follow through. I was well aware that he would do whatever it took to drag me down, but the thought of losing Kim scared me beyond belief. She was my safe haven; I didn't know what to do without her. Of course, I believed every word he said to me that morning. I cried, and then I did something really brave… I called Kim.

I told her everything. I told her I'd lied and that I was struggling to leave him. I told her that he knew where she lived and had been over before. I also told her about his threats. I waited on the other end of the phone for her to kick me out and end our friendship and much to my surprise she said:

"Oh honey, I would never choose his side over you. Let's get a security system for the house now that he knows where we live".

This is when I truly began to learn what true unconditional love looked and felt like. Kim had my back no matter what. Her love was unshakable. She loved me whether I was thriving in life or struggling to get out of bed, it didn't matter.

Her love was all encompassing, supportive and strong. She didn't judge me for seeing 'him'. She allowed me the space to fumble in my growth while she held a stable space for my heart to show up. I cannot put into words what sort of a healing effect it has to have people in your life that see you and love you no-matter-what. She got it.

Kim was never mad at me. She worried and she cared deeply, but anger was not her style. Booking us massages and giving me small gifts, that was Kim's style. This gave me strength. He lost a tiny bit of power over my heart when I knew I had an unwavering tribe member by my side.

Every time I fell, Kim was there to pick me and wait for me to dust off my own knees. She believed in me like I had never seen anyone believe in someone. She was put onto my path for a reason. She saved my life.

I remember nights of intense internal pain, while living with Kim, before I told her the truth that I was still seeing him, behind her back. I was lying to everyone at that time; held a dirty secret too shameful to say aloud. My soul knew this was not good for me. By this point the drama was miserable and intense, the layers of dynamics just piled up like rotting trash.

At the same time as his threats to disclose our secret to Kim, and my confession to Kim, and her acceptance of me for who I was, a glimmer of hope appeared in my professional life and brightened the days.

I began working at INLIV, an integrated health care business which offers a unique blend of services. I loved being there. Their philosophy aligned with my own in terms of wanting to help others heal.

But on the relationship front, things went from bad to worse. He continued to harass me. I changed my number.

Yes! Changed. My. Number.

Kim and I headed to the lake for the long weekend. I had my new phone number and I felt great about my new job. But the severe case of relationship dysfunction accompanied me. And so, abandoning all things proactive and healthy-boundary-like, I caved and called him.

Yes! From. The. New. Number.

And the vine of Anguish smiled. And my feet became more mired in the swamp.

He sent me a series of messages calling me a whore, and sent pictures of his house-cleaner who I thought resembled an escort. The accompanying message instructed me to 'go be a whore, that's what you're good at anyway. Here's my date tonight.'

The names continued. Dirt bag. Useless Whore. Loser. A 28 year old loser because I'd been living with Kim. He said I'd failed at everything I'd tried in my life. He predicted I'd fail at everything I would try in my future. He stated that Kim was a whore too. He sent more pictures of other women. He told me I should hurt as badly as he was hurting.

August 29, 2012

A lot has happened. He and I made an attempt (to make the relationship work) and once again he freaked out at me. After spending three months with friends and family, and working on myself, I found him to be extremely controlling, and I ended up feeling quite isolated.

Anyway, today I'm learning that I need to reinvent myself—I want to discover who I am and what I want in my life.

→►═◉ ◉═◄←

August 30, 2012

I don't know how to let go of him – I won't move on until I do… but I keep feeling sucked back in, keep feeling like it will change. It's never been good – I don't get it.

I've lost myself, my power, my voice and my passion. I'm lost, not grounded, and I have NO IDEA what to do about it. I feel like since I got home two years ago I have accomplished nothing. I'm embarrassed by my existence. I've thought about suicide – it's not just him, it's everything. It's the anxiety I feel, the lack of career and money. No direction or stability. I'm not sure how much strength I have – I walk around in a daze; a passion-less daze.

→►═◉ ◉═◄←

August 31, 2012

Here I am again: lost. Why do I keep allowing him to take my power? He's truly so mean to me. He hangs up on me, controls me – he's mad because I am having beer with a girlfriend tonight.

WHAT THE FUCK?!?

He leaves me Saturday, ignores my 30 calls Sunday, spends the week texting me – love texts and hate texts, then expects that I want to go for wine and oysters with him, and when I have plans, he freaks out at me.

WHY CAN'T I LET GO?

→⊨◎ ◎⊨←

September the fucking second, 2012

Saturday morning I woke to 20 missed texts from him – he was having yet another freak out at me, calling me:

"The worst fuck he's ever had"

"Whore"

"Broke ass"

"Dirt bag"

"You're a joke to them all"

I was a mess Saturday. He came over in tears and I immediately took him back, even though he sent me two pictures of the girls he's been on dates with.

WHAT'S WRONG WITH ME?

→⊨◎ ◎⊨←

Journal Entry: Dateless

"You're single now so more guys will get lucky and I pay"

"Not such a stand up girl"

"Here is your concert ticket" (with a picture of the girl he took instead of me)

"Fuck you"

"Be a whore"

"You're a joke"

"Worst fuck ever"

"I do not love you"

"You're worthless"

"You're useless"

"You offer nothing"

"You drag me down"

"You're just trying to fight"
"You're just not a happy person"
"Not independent"
"You're not worth it"
"It's you, not me"

I know, I can hardly believe it when I read it, let alone consider incorporating it into this book, but it has to be here to show the complete and utter psychological phenomenon of the abuser and, more importantly, an abused mindset.

CHAPTER 13

One. Phone. Call.
2012

I SPENT PRETTY much every day—part of September and into October—basically living with PH, together, as in a couple. But not a normal couple.

He showed his support by coming to some of my runs to watch me cross the finish line, but this brought logistical difficulties to the forefront. My family and friends were often there. My family and friends hated him. This further isolated me from those I cherished. Trapped in even more drama than I'd ever experienced, I found it difficult to move forward. To add to the stress, both Kim and Andrea received promotions and shared each would be moving away. I made plans to move out of Kim's house; my sister and I found a cute little apartment to share.

Quite possibly, the only thing that kept me whole was that I was thrilled not to suffer any injuries during an extended spell of intense training while I did a lot of running and prepared for a half-marathon.

But before I moved, Kim and I sat at the kitchen table. She told me that I needed help, and I knew her words were the absolute truth. Therapy was inevitable. There was no arguing with her, even though therapy was the last thing I wanted. I had no idea who to go and see, so I said a prayer to 'God'—the guy in the sky with whom I had a 'silent treatment, not sure I believe in you' relationship.

Kim found the number. The therapist's, not God's.

And I called. The therapist, not God.

The 'other' last thing I wanted was to NOT be paired with a male therapist.

I was paired with a male therapist.

We spoke on the phone and I explained that this breakup made me think of my dead father, and that I was overwhelmed by sadness.

I told him it had been five months since the fateful fight and moving in with Kim and I was no closer to clarity or healing—in fact, I was further away life had become completely unmanageable, and the darkness was swallowing me. I didn't know who I was, what I loved or even how to feel joy. I was stuck in the merry-go-round of breaking up and secretly sneaking around with PH.

I shared that people in my life had suggested that I file a police report against PH; there was worry in the eyes of the humans in my life.

The therapist put me at ease during that phone call.

And, though I worked hard not to show how hurt, lost, and terrified I felt about everything, I came to realize life was 'officially' too much for me to handle. I realized I had found a counsellor. Embarrassed, humiliated, lost, and confused, it took a lot of effort and self-talk for me to show up to his office, but I believed I would die if I did not get help—thoughts of dying were overwhelming at this point.

October 2012 saw a broken, shattered, empty me sitting across from a therapist named Marcus. I sat 'on the couch' across from a man who appeared slightly older than me. Shame filled my every cell; a shell of a human wearing a purple Lululemon jacket. I remember the exact tights and the runners. My hair was in a ponytail. My skin was dry. Frail and underweight, my spirit was dead.

I looked him in the eye and told him I was there for two reasons:

to find my spark

to save my relationship with PH

After all that had happened it truly pained me to admit, out loud, that I actually wanted to be with a monster of a human being. And so began the long journey to healthy.

—◦—

It is so easy to see it now, total clarity in that the situation was devastatingly unhealthy, for both of us. It is so easy to see, now, the sheer lack of self-love I had. But back then I could not see the map that would point me in the direction of home. Its legend was a blank black square. I was lost in a perpetual night in the city of me; drowning in darkness.

CHAPTER 14

Zen and the Art of Dysfunction

2012

ONE OF THE first things Marcus, the therapist, told me was that a broken heart is like an initiation into adulthood. I liked hearing that because of the next part he shared: that, through this initiation, I would get to choose who I wanted to be.

One requires a broken heart for initiation into adulthood.

October 11, 2012

I started seeing a counsellor on Tuesday. It was hard. I cried a lot. I have come to realize that over the past two years, I have really lost myself. I don't have the beliefs I used to have. I don't do the things I love. I have become overwhelmed; in anxiety and fear based thinking.

I decided that I need some space from him (PH) - some space to figure ME out. I'm not at all ready to walk away from him, but I need some ME time. I was scared to talk to him, scared he would be mad - I wanted to suggest one date night and one gym night - and it turned into a fight. He was not supportive.

If I knew he was going to work on things I would be so happy. I don't think he is going to work on things. But why do I keep waiting?

THIS IS SO FUCKED UP!!!! AGHHHHH.

I told him last night that I needed some space. I told him there is NOTHING wrong with that and that it's NORMAL. He got mad. He said, "Now you're back to you and your friends and all I do is chase you."

REALITY: For the past month I have spent almost every day with him and I have ditched ALL friends, family, and me time.

THERE IS NOTHING WRONG WITH ME TIME. IT'S A RIGHT, NOT A FUCKING PRIVILEGE. I'M SO FUCKING MAD. I HATE THIS. HE IS SO UNREASONABLE AND I'M FUCKING HOOKED—WHAT A LOSER I AM.

Initially, in counselling, Marcus had me focus on what I wanted. And I knew what I wanted.

To be strong, value focused, unwilling to settle.
To have deep sense of self love and respect.
To create a fun life with meaningful relationships.
A career in which my life's work makes a difference.
To be quirky, outgoing, and strong willed.
To have a meaningful relationship with spirituality and intuition.
To be the kind of person that knows she deserves great things.

But my biggest fear was that I had been losing myself. I confided to Marcus that:

I didn't have cool goals anymore.
I didn't talk about spirituality.
I didn't spend my time with friends.
I didn't coach or read self-help books.
I didn't contact friends overseas.

I expressed that I knew I was the most important thing I had, but that I was slipping away. I realized that I needed to really focus on self-love.

I wanted to learn to take care of myself like I would a best friend.

I needed and wanted to set boundaries on how much I saw 'PH' so that I could create space for my own self-love and clarity.

I hoped 'PH'—the crazy man in my life—would understand my needs.

I hoped 'PH' knew that I loved him.

I hoped 'PH' knew that I want our relationship to work.

But, I knew the SELF had to be repaired in order for the couple part to work.

I was so mad at life. So hurt. But I expressed I was ready to face this hurt and address the things I want and need.

I told Marcus that I loved: reading, writing, running, yoga, A Course In Miracles, emailing Sally, Cill, Stevie, Julia, Elena, Jax, and Han, planning trips, playing with my dog, reading about nutrition, cooking healthy foods, and meditating.

One of the last questions Marcus the counsellor asked me—after directing me to close my eyes—was this:

"Kori, I want you to complete this statement: if PH were here, the one thing I would want him to know is…"

I started to cry. Then I completed the sentence:

"If PH was here, the one thing I would want him to know is… **that I love him very much.**"

→➡ ⬅←

In my journal I acknowledged the need to work on boundaries, but I had no clue what a boundary was. The 'boundaries' I had in my relationship with him (PH) were like lines in the sand; easily washed away by the next wave. I constantly compromised.

All the horrible words in my diagram—outside that boundary circle— remained my reality. The healthy words inside the circle simply didn't exist. It didn't matter how many times I wrote them, or how many internal conversations I had, or how many times I spoke to others about what I wanted, or how many discussions took place in couple-therapy sessions, no waking moment of my life matched the healthy boundaries I'd stated I wanted.

I am an extrovert by nature; I have zero doubt about that. I absolutely thrive around human beings. I have always loved and been fascinated by the human race; we are an interesting species and I love loving us—as in everyone on the planet.

I love talking to people and listening to their life experiences. I love crowds, festivals, and dancing. I adore being the center of attention. Loudness and chaos are comforting—growing up in a big family, the dynamics were close and colourful. My best friends were my siblings, my Mum, my cousins, my Gram, and my Aunts.

In the history of my relationships—other than my Aussie sailor—I did not embody a single identity, rather, I always slipped into another being's realm of human operation. I was always Kori and _____. I required another person's name inserted after the 'and'. Though individualism was and is important to me, I had no idea how to accomplish it.

I did not understand where I ended and another human began. Though I wanted to be 'Kori involved in something wonderful', I deferred to becoming an appendage of someone in my life.

The relationship that I eventually left, the one in which I totally lost my sense of self, was a dramatic example of merging with another human. Looking back, I can see how I stifled my intuition, suppressing it in order to maintain an illusion of love.

Compromising my values to be with him was a choice I made without understanding why I made it.

For example: steroids. I don't care what research exists to justify steroids, I do not agree with their use. I have never agreed with their use. And yet, it was still somehow okay that 'he' used them. I placed my opinion in a box, sealed it, and placed it on a shelf as if 'out of sight' removed it from my reality.

And, each time I shut out my values and beliefs—attacked my value system—I grew more distant in my heart. The sad thing was, this distance was not a void between myself and PH, but a chasm between me and me. Each time I ignored intuition, I betrayed my own divine sense of self. I was the one who fell deeper and deeper into a mistrust of self.

We teach people how to treat us; if I didn't value myself, why would anyone else?

PH did not value me. He did not value himself. I did not value myself.

In counselling, I began to learn that I had a lot of anger from my Father's passing. Not only did I hold anger toward my Father for dying, I blamed God. I didn't trust the universe. Of course, until I began uncovering layers of myself in counselling, I didn't know this. But, through counselling, I became aware that I'd not had the space to properly grieve. This set up a hostile battle inside me.

"I am the adult, you are the child" were words I often heard. Adulthood meant respect, childhood meant no respect. I disagreed with this as a child; still deeply disagree with this.

Although I hold all the compassion in the world for my Mum—for I cannot even imagine how it must have been for her at the time of my Dad's passing, and I know that she did the very best she could—early days of therapy helped me see that while I loved my Mum so much, my anger over childhood experiences existed: justified or not.

I would move forward from those first sessions, courageously facing and processing the anger—over time.

Once one acknowledges her anger, and understands why the anger is there, she can't pretend it isn't.

CHAPTER 15

Little Kori

MEET LITTLE KORI, she is my inner child. An innocent one.

I'd met Little Kori when I was in my early twenties, when I'd studied life-coaching. Therefore, throughout the chaos of my life that followed, I knew that in order for me to heal I was going to have to do a few things:

1. Get Little Kori to like me, trust me, or at least look at me.
2. Address current Kori's anger and cold-hearted coping techniques that included distancing people.

I would eventually learn that my most important job—my first priority—was to protect Little Kori. I would also learn that this would be harder than one would think.

Protecting Little Kori would require actual effort, just like in a real relationship with another human. Little Kori was like a rescue dog with her tail between her legs. She was terrified and mistrusting. Slow and steady care, with unlimited patience, would be required to understand, gain her trust, and ultimately protect Little Kori.

Sadly, in undertaking the work for this process, I discovered I had virtually no patience with Little Kori. Quick to get angry at Little Kori, I would make things worse. I would forget about her—on a regular basis—choosing abuse and drama. And because of that neglect, she further mistrusted me.

She made it clear to me that, without her trust, I had no future as a functional, self-loving adult. My self-love would be born through the development of my abilities to love Little Kori. There would be no way to hurry this relationship;

she required time, and when I pressured her she would retreat to the corner, and I would lose any connection we'd made Not only would I be back to square one, I would have created even deeper wounds to address.

The other truth that enveloped me in darkness, which, ironically, made me grateful I didn't have to look at Little Kori, was that I'd denied Little Kori the space to process emotions. At six years old, she'd been robbed of her sense of joy. Over the years, I'd told her she was stupid, fat, and useless. I put her in that corner to which she often retreated. The reason she would not look at me was my own fault; there was no one else to blame. I had abandoned her many moons ago, and had since forgotten that she was cold, alone, scared, (and had been for more than two decades). Darkness does that.

No fucking wonder she didn't trust me.

It was like I was stuck between multiple worlds. There was the wounded part of my psyche—Little Kori—who feared abandonment; she missed her father, her growth had been stunted, she was numb, deeply lonely, and sad.

And there was another part of my 'adult self', who appeared to be mimicking a vengeful, loud teenager, rebelling against all of the fucking rules, and having a 'hate-on' for all the wounded parts of self—which was basically the whole self.

In addition, there was 'me' the witness. A me who was scared to look at the aspects of my 'self' because I had no clue how to embody all the parts of my 'human-ness'. What I knew for certain was that part of me was distrusting and deeply hurt, and part of me was fucking pissed and extremely angry.

CHAPTER 16

Ursula

MEET URSULA. SHE is my spunk, my high energy, and my creative force. When undernourished, suppressed, or ignored she is my addiction to drama, my reason for having to numb out. She is pure rage. To say she gets fucking pissed would be an understatement.

I met Ursula around the same time I met Little Kori—when I was in my early twenties, studying life-coaching.

In an assignment to meet my 'ego' there was a requirement to name and personify it.

The objective was for each participant to allow his or her ego the opportunity to communicate by having the ego write a letter to its host. This way, it was explained that each student would get to know the ever present negative voice in his or her head. Back then, little did I know that, years later, while in an extremely abusive and dysfunctional relationship, I would actively work on getting to know every intimate detail about my ego.

Ursula behaved exactly like the same-named character in 'The Little Mermaid'. She'd slink quietly into my life and take a gentle hold, then squeeze, until it was no longer a light touch but a firm grip over my entire being. This would leave me deeply out of balance, and completely open to dysfunction.

A mystery to me, Ursula had the power to transform into an enchanting persona who fit perfectly into my good intentions, only to steal my voice, bring me back to her cave under the sea, and morph into her true monstrous self. It was in those inky, depths that I'd be held captive.

Ursula visited often. She incited and cheered on a rebellious, detestable attitude. I despised her. She was so insidiously sneaky. I wanted to kill her. I worked hard to hold her back, but she'd show up when she felt like it, wreak havoc, and leave only after total destruction had been accomplished.

Ursula made my thoughts race. She was devious, taking possession of me by 'talking goals and to-dos'. She'd lure me with vision boards and dizzy me with affirmations—she loved watching me race to meet success only to be stood up. She was positively tipsy when I went into a cocaine-like high-speed mindset in a mad-dash to achieve, achieve, achieve—to complete life tasks. Then she'd vomit all over whatever I'd hoped for.

The aftermath was like a bad hangover. She never cleaned up.

In therapy, with Marcus, I trimmed back some leaves, pulled her out from behind the twisty vine, squished her onto a slide, and put her under the microscope—I'd always loved science.

The closer I looked, the less omnipotent she appeared. She was less like an inky blob—a cartridge failure on an otherwise impeccable manuscript—and more like a recognizable shape.

As I focussed the powerful lens on her, she took the form of a defiant adolescent. A scrawny teenager, maybe sixteenish: denim cutoffs; a sleeveless plaid shirt, cropped by having tied the shirt-ends in a bow, revealed her navel; red cowboy boots she called shit-kickers. She was topped off by a mangled cowboy hat. With one hand on her hip, her other held out toward me, middle finger pointed straight up in the air, she stood her ground. Unintimidated by being the subject of a study, she kept the 'bird' high, and shouted at me: "FUCK OFF".

It was not that scientific; it was more like science fiction.

Therapy allowed me to study her in detail. She ran the shit show in my heart. She drank and partied way too hard and way too often. She coped with one night stands and abusive relationships. She had a loud mouth and was rough around the edges. She wanted nothing to do with authenticity.

Seeing her in all her glory—totally magnified—brought home a deep understanding of why I often showed up in life so cold and so distant; I even had an ex- boyfriend who had lovingly nicknamed me 'ice queen'. I knew I had rage, but where it came from had made no sense until I understood Ursula.

Sometimes when I close my eyes and think about Ursula, the Goddess of Shit, she appears wearing her rebellious, skanky outfit and tells me to fuck off…

but I have learned to apply self-compassion even to the parts of myself that I wish would be different and, furthermore, I have learned to deeply respect and appreciate the crevices of my soul that seem a bit fucked up.

When I was firmly entrenched in dysfunction—a place I call the soul swamp—the idea of death was very appealing. It is possible that, on some level, Ursula's dysfunctional coping techniques of numbing may have bought me time, and saved my life.

It is the darkest parts of the soul that need the most acceptance and love.

Chapter 17

Enemy Territory and Treaties

2012

"What do you want to say or do to Ursula?" my therapist, Marcus, asked.

"Kill her." I replied without hesitation.

He firmly told me, "Eliminating parts of your psyche is not allowed; you will have to learn to live with her."

"What the fuck. It's my psyche; can't I do what I want?" I said.

Well as it turns out, no, I couldn't just remain wanting to kill her, because the more I hated Ursula—Queen of everything contemptuous—the louder she became in my life. And, Oh-My-God, once this sleeping dragon was awakened there was NO shutting her up. I would have to—for my life's sake—figure out how to deal with her; how to live with her.

By hating Ursula, I became the darkest parts of her. I needed to learn to fully understand Ursula's role, in order to channel her energy and use it for positive means. In other words, I had to learn how to honour all of the fragmented parts of my own self.

The more I engaged with Ursula's destructive powers, the more I dishonoured myself, and the more I would drink or use cocaine. Though I had used it infrequently in the past—in an experimental 'come-on try it' party atmosphere, the mood around alcohol and drugs shifted from party participation to 'use to numb'. The more volatile I became, the more times I'd return to PH, a man who was flat-out abusive. I'd lash out at PH, screaming and yelling. This led to mutual violence. Then I'd get silent and sulk.

The deeper I sunk into Ursula's murky depths, the more Little Kori withdrew.

Ursula created havoc and the package that appeared as 'me' became completely unmanageable: drugs, abuse, drinking, self-harm, suicidal thoughts, depression, debilitating anxiety, long bouts of insomnia, night terrors, rage at myself and most humans who crossed my path. I was impossible to be around; I was experiencing all-encompassing-anger

I hated myself. All I wanted to do was escape.

It turned out that Ursula was trying to communicate, and I did eventually translate the words: "Help me, please. I'm begging you to love me."

Little Kori was trying to communicate also, demanding more and more from me. She required consistency before letting me near. And, as long as I was fighting to block out Ursula, the less I could provide Little Kori.

Over time, I would learn, there were in fact ways to honour Ursula's spunky edge. I would learn that this part of my soul loved to write, and loved to stand up for a cause—she would be the side of me that used her voice for the voiceless, the side that pushed to speak in public, for goodness. Nourishing this side of me was absolutely essential to my balance and wellbeing.

And, in honouring Ursula's spunky edge, Little Kori responded positively.

CHAPTER 18

Reruns

2012

October 16, 2012

I voiced my boundaries to 'him' on Friday, and opened up the conversation, asking him for his opinions. He freaked out; started throwing the Stampede issue in my face. On Saturday I told him to stop texting me. By Sunday night I had 30 missed text messages. He called me a whore and a hooker; said I was probably waking up with another random guy because, 'that's how I fix problems'. He is so mean to me. I'm trying really hard to stay strong. Being treated like this is not okay. It's really hard.

⇥▦ ▦⇤

October 28, 2012

I break down in tears when I hear songs. My heart still hurts so much. I told him that I need a month to focus on me, with no communication. He said he'd respect that. But he is still texting; they are all really nice, but, it is still texting.

I'm starting to glimpse traces of myself. I'm starting to laugh again. I feel passion toward life. I'm making friends at work. Even my job seems to be opening up with more possibilities.

The future is scaring me a little less.

Then he texts.

⇥▦ ▦⇤

October 28, 2012 (later)

Counselling was really good on Friday. Marcus and I got talking about childhood stuff, and Dad dying, and what I learned was that I have some anger... a lot of anger. I focus some of it on my childhood. I didn't have enough experience, back then, to understand boundaries. Even now, I don't have a decent grasp on boundaries with others. I have to start working on a relationship with my inner-child – start nurturing myself and learn to trust. I cope by distancing.

I seem to be rebelling – he is still texting me – the same bipolar bullshit. It's actually pretty scary. He literally has no respect for me. It's a rollercoaster being in this and it's really hard to get out.

I'm going to have a couple of low key, quiet weekends and re-center myself.

⟶▭ ▭⟵

October 29, 2012

At three in the morning I got a text from him saying he left something on the balcony for me. He left me shoes – a new pair of runners for my half marathon. He left a card, too. Why won't he respect my space? Why is he so mean? And why won't he let me go?

I have made new friends. I talk to them a lot. In particular I enjoy *Stampede Guy's* thoughts about life. He seems grounded and connected to the universe. I like how he treats me – kind and respectful.

I think Marcus is right about the fact that I do not have good (or any) boundaries; something I really have to work on. I think I hold a lot of anger. I am confused about a lot of things. I walk away before I even try to stand my ground.

Everything feels so confusing and overwhelming – I just go numb. I actually feel really sad. Lost. Alone. I have so much to face and I don't even really know how to start.

⟶▭ ▭⟵

Oct 30, 2012

Homework from Marcus: I'm supposed to journal about that little girl that I left behind 22 years ago, I'm meant to relate to her and see what it is that she needs. I'm meant to create a bond and show her that she can trust my lead.

I don't know how to do this.

All that I can come up are three things: 1. How cute she was - based on pictures that I have seen. 2. How terribly sad I am - still to this day. 3. How angry I am. If I don't feel that heartstring being pulled I mostly feel this sense of being distant, cold, and pissed off. My heart can quickly swing in and out of compassion and tender to anger, even rage.

I'm so mad that he died.

Thinking back to that little girl, the only way I can describe this is to say that one day things were great, and the next all I see is her little self, and big blue eyes, and long hair, and she's standing in a desert – alone. No one is around, there is no sound other than the wind and all she can sense (I can tell she can sense it) is that for all eternity there will be an endless pit of sand.

She's not crying, she has a deep longing in her eyes, but no tears. I guess at this point she's gotta dust off and figure out how to keep going. She's hurt though – she seems to have a lot of depth, but it's all hidden in her long hair blowing in the wind, her determined little face, and her eyes. She seems to stand there, her dress blowing in the wind, for what seems like forever.

It seems like she is stuck in a complete daze And all of a sudden she seems to 'come back', take a deep breath, and start walking. I'm not sure she knows where she is going. I don't know how she could – but it's almost as if the stark surroundings have no effect on her.

It's like she is encased in an invisible, hard shield – nothing can touch her. I think she's mad. I think she feels very alone; very pissed off that she has been left all alone – so very alone.

A…a…a…and I'm crying.

I am longing for a certain love, (one that little girl needs). I am wanting that sort of protection so much. But I do not trust that there will be any, so if any shows up, I will not believe in love, not one tiny little bit. I'm just so angry. So angry. I'm mad that it happened. I'm mad that I am STILL stuck in it. I don't even know what "it" is.

I feel like I have always had pressure to lift my chin and see the next step, see the positive, the gift. But, little Kori is hurt, feels abandoned, and believes she had to grow up to soon. She's mad about the whole 'children respect their elders, period'. She's pissed - and convinced - that NOTHING felt safe.

This is starting to sound like a sob story. I think I'm done for now.

⟶🔑 🔑⟵

October 31, 2012

The day when I don't cry, will be a big deal. This process is painful.

It's only just now starting to become clear to me the control and impact he has had on my life. I've spent time over the last couple of days reconnecting with people with whom I'd had relationships. I thought those relationships were lost. Maybe they're not.

I lost everything being with him – self-love, self-worth, the desire to travel, passion, spark, friends – and for what? He lied to me, kept secrets from me, belittled me, called me names...

HE REALLY HURT ME.

He is texting me daily. I'm not responding. I told him to leave me alone, and he isn't. It's scaring me.

I kept taking mental vacations into my history, reflecting and then daydreaming. Projecting goals, became a regular pastime. Many related to running.

Some of my favourite runs took place in the winter; cold and dark with no one on the path. There was a magic about the solitude and darkness. In my winter running days, I worked at Lululemon, which was good for me because I was with my 'people'—the kind who detox, run marathons, and open spin studios.

They eat organic food and care about their health. These people work on self-improvement. I lived in two realities: the one at work with healthy people who continually moved forward in joy and celebration of the human condition, and the one at home—totally opposite.

I remember going into work some mornings, massively hungover outrageously swollen eyes caused by screaming matches and uncontrollable tears the previous night. It only served to remind me how much I wanted to be one of those people with healthy goals. Though it upset me that I had no idea how to get what they had—so I hated the job. Deep down, I knew I was made for healing.

CHAPTER 19

Let It Snow, Let Me Grow, Let Me Go

2012 YEAR END

In November 2012 I ran my first ever half-marathon. A life accomplishment. I began to feel like I was fitting in at work. Though I had no money saved, I felt some hope. I didn't speak to PH for the whole month. It was as if I could breathe for the first time. Counselling became my sacred place. I felt like 'me'. I even felt like I could flirt with others using the old 'spark' I'd had. I began to think I might be worthy.

But then I broke the 'him cleanse'. What followed were the predictable ups and downs. He'd text-abuse, then be sorry and say he would change. I struggled with trying to cut it off. I missed Andrea and Kim a lot.

Counselling was the one place that provided clarity. Work also gave me a sense of worth. INLIV was a good place to begin a career to help others. I began to think about going to school again. I began looking forward to a New Year, 2013, as people do when a 'January' clean start is on the horizon.

I resolved that although I was not where I once thought I'd be—successful career, home, family and finances—I had done a good job of LIVING. I'd travelled the world, lived outside Canada, had enjoyed a long-term relationship. I felt it was truly time to surrender to serious growth. I felt committed to getting well and creating a life I deserved.

November 20, 2012

I have started to feel a renewal – experiencing a small amount of hope and happiness. I'm starting to see how totally dysfunctional and dangerous he and I are. I have been processing a lot of anger and dealing with it in counselling.

I walk a tightrope every day – if I fall, I believe it will kill me or cause irreversible damage. He is my 'heroin', and I am craving a hit.

Under all of my anger, I am completely broken hearted. It's so hard to remain open, the walls come up so fast.

I went on a blind date on Saturday. Super nice guy, I might see him again – we'll see.

→⎯◎ ◎⎯←

December 5, 2012

I've been listening to the book 'The Shadow Effect', which dives into the shadow side of our psyche – I'm learning that I am actually quiet ashamed about who I am and where my life is at – money, career, education, direction, and purpose.

I've been working on slowing down and reconnecting with my feminine side. I recall a time in my life that I practiced yoga, meditated, devoured books, wanted to be an international speaker and spiritual leader – where did that girl go?

He emailed me again today – I fucking miss him. He does not deserve my thoughts, love or emotion.

ALL I WANT TO DO IS EMAIL HIM.

I WANT A HUG.

I WANT TO KNOW IT WILL BE OK, THAT IT WAS ALL A BAD DREAM.

BABY – WAKE ME UP, IM SCARED.

I MISS YOU. PLEASE, WAKE ME UP – I MISS YOU.

I MISS YOU.

I'm so sad and anxious – I don't want to keep living like this.

＊＊＊

December 8, 2012

I had more counselling on Thursday with Marcus. It's helpful.

I have not worked out in a week – my guilty conscience is huge. I'm trying to slow down and feel and listen. I hope life starts to make sense one day. I don't want to feel so lost. Marcus thinks that not only did I NOT grow in the past two years with 'him' (PH), but that I actually regressed. It's a very sad realization to discover that two years of my life have been wasted.

I went to bed thinking about him (PH), and I woke with him on my mind. It's bizarre how much I miss him – the only thing that keeps me from contacting him is the fact that Marcus would be disappointed.

My homework is to continue working on the 'feel'.

I have an incredible amount of sadness in my heart right now. When I touch my hand to my heart it's a river of tears – unexplained. I don't know where it's all coming from. I'm trying to stay with it, and not attach names or stories to it.

My job right now is simply to observe.

＊＊＊

December 9, 2012

I saw him last night at a pub – he was on a date. That hurt. Then, in my foolish drunken state I fucking called him at four thirty this morning. I feel like a failure. I did however have a conversation with him tonight. I told him to leave me alone, told him that he is a manipulative abusive man. It actually felt good to stand up for myself. I

told him that he left me a shell of a person. I told him I am in counselling and working hard, and picking up the pieces. He said he was
'sorry'. I didn't believe him and told him that. He cried. I told him
it's too fucking late for tears.

→►═◉ ◉═◄←

December 10, 2012

It's weird; I have woken with the exact same anxiety I used to have
with him. The world is grey. My stomach is in knots.

Really interesting.

I'm going to really focus on self-protection.

OMG, the texts are starting again. I cannot let this happen – I feel
totally drained.

→►═◉ ◉═◄←

Dear Universe,

I want to make a difference in this lifetime in the lives of others. I
want to help them return to love.

I want a job I love – a wellness sanctuary, near the ocean.

I want a husband and an over-the-top romance.

I want to be loved and respected.

My husband will be my best friend.

I want a family, to take care of people, to cook, bake, and nurture.

I want to travel the whole world.

I want to sail.

I want a garden and a compost.

I want fresh flowers.

I want abundance, love, joy and peace.

Despite the desperation, I could still articulate what I wanted. I hadn't lost
sight of it. Yet the learning curve was steep. I had to manage Ursula and
Little Kori.

December 12, 2012

I caved and saw him last night. He stopped by to talk. I knew it wouldn't help, but at the same time, (I hoped) maybe it would.

This is all so intense. So hard. I had no idea anything could ever feel like this.

So many red flags, and yet such massive hope... and denial.

I felt like I've been holding heavy flood gates closed, and last night I just fell.

I yelled at him – told him how horribly he's hurt me. Then he came in. I cried. He held me. It felt so good. I never wanted to let go. I so badly want to believe his words, his touch... I think it's all a lie though – there are so many unanswered questions.

I'm starting to actually wonder if he is a sociopath.

I hope I have not undone all of my hard work. I want to get through this – I think I am depressed.

God, please help me.

⇢▬◉ ◎▬⇠

December 17, 2012

Lately, all the days seem to hurt a lot. Maybe today hurts because I spent the weekend with him. I miss him so much. It's so sad for me to hear all of his promises about how much he loves me, and to hear his promises to change and work on things and then never does. I want so badly to believe him, but he's unlikely to change. It's something that I have to accept.

Gotta just focus on working on my own self.

⇢▬◉ ◎▬⇠

December 19, 2012

I have never been so sad in my life. Marcus says it's deeper than 'him' – that it's years of sadness coming up.

I feel depressed.

I'm tired.
I lie around a lot.

→▣ ▣←

December 20, 2012

I had counselling last night. Marcus said I was in the worst shape he has seen me – he said my condition is directly related to my connection with 'him' (PH). He explained that there is a deep wisdom in me that knows that this (being with PH) is wrong, therefore, in order for me to be with 'him' I basically leave my body and become unconscious.

Marcus shared that he felt I was very fragmented.

It was a weird session. I could feel myself popping in and out of myself (my consciousness) Marcus said he could 'see' it. It took us a few hours to centre me and restore balance.

→▣ ▣←

December 26, 2012

(In a merry effing Christmas present to myself kind of way)

Christmas is over – Thank God.

I'm really struggling in my life. I don't know why I can't seem to let go of him. The whole 'can't seem to let go of him' is getting old.

He drunk texted me on Friday again (before Christmas) - he was really mean; I fucked him the next day (Saturday).

WHAT THE FUCK?

Will I ever be happy again?

I don't even want to live

No, I will heal.

→▣ ▣←

December 27, 2012

So, Christmas week, on Saturday, he got drunk – had another awful freak out at me.

Sunday he was crying and saying sorry.

Monday he spent most of the day with me telling me how all he wants is Christmas together, blah, blah, blah.

Tuesday was all 'love' texts. He misses me. Calls me.

Wednesday he was clearly mad for some reason; barely talked to me. Ignored my love messages

Thursday: TOTAL SILENCE

AM I HIS FUCKING PUPPET??? Hot. Cold. Hot. Cold. Love. Hate. Love. Hate

IT'S A FUCKING JOKE!!!!

Marcus says to cry until I have no more tears left for 'him'.

I just re-read my journal – This whole thing is a vicious cycle. He says mean and unforgivable things to me – comes over crying with empty promises of change – does nothing to change – I feel bad for him, I miss him, I take him back – he freaks out and is back to being mean.

Tomorrow Marcus and I are going to talk more about Ursula and disassociation. Again, Marcus explains that in order for me to be with 'him' (PH), I literally have to leave my body.

And, when people disassociate too often, then the mind becomes trained to deal with hurt in this way: in a state of disassociation. At that point, is there a way back?

⊷▬◉ ◉▬◐⊶

December 28, 2012

Dear Kori,

When he texts, please remember that he: does not care, lies, fucks whores, calls you names, hits you, and also remember that your friends and family hate him.

Oh, yeah, on December 26th he randomly quit contacting you after he spilled his "I Love You" lies.

FUCKER.

→═◉ ◉═←

December 30, 2012

I know its best that he is suddenly ignoring me – but I would be lying if I didn't admit that it hurts an incredible amount. All last week was gifts and promises, then he fucks off on a vacation with friends and totally ignores me.

Other than having started counselling, there was little difference between 2011 and 2012 year's end. There'd been another year of wear on my physical and emotional self—like a set of tires that had completed one half of a cross country round trip—I still had to have enough tread to find my way home.

10, 9, 8, 7, 6, 5, 4, 3, 2, Unhappy fucking New Year.

CHAPTER 20

Write Me to the End of Love

2013

January 7, 2013

I spent all weekend with him again.

Maybe rather than clinging to solutions, the way getting over a broken heart is simply to accept that right now it just really, really hurts.

-->◖=◐ ◑=◗<--

Journal entry: undated, but titled: Reflections of 2012.

Maybe I'm being dramatic, and although I know things can always be worse, I believe that 2012 has been the single worst year of my life. So here I am... exploring the abundant pain of the swamp. The Soul Swamp. For me this experience is almost unbearable. It's so dark and so black.

It feels like a hole - a never-ending hole - that just goes deeper and deeper and deeper. Apparently this is the way to light – I guess it's like the Phoenix (bird) that burns in the ashes and is reborn.

There are times like now (and last night) that I cancel all plans and just crash on the bed and cry. I have never slept so much in my life, or had such a desire to be alone in a dark room. I don't know if it's normal. I used to be such a positive person, people say I am, but I feel like a dark cloud.

My heart just hurts. It hurts so much that it's hard to breathe and it's hard to 'stay' with a healing plan. I want to escape; sometimes I do anything to escape. I have fallen and seen him, I have drunk so much that I've made dumb choices. I think dark suicidal thoughts – it's all incredibly overwhelming.

I'm told that it's ok, that this is normal, that I need to go through all of this. I trust that – somehow it feels right – but it's frustrating and painful.

I think that my sadness is probably a lot more than just this breakup, this seven-month-long breakup – but wow, do I ever miss him a TON. I tried so very hard to make it work. I really, really loved that guy. I loved his safe arms, I loved the idea of marriage and kids, and taking care of a family. That was so new to me – and I can't imagine it with anyone else. Maybe one day I will heal. Or maybe I will never ever get over him. I always thought I was worth the fight – I believe that love was worth the fight. Maybe it wasn't love?

Maybe he just does not care. Who knows? All I know is that I wish with every ounce of my being that he would step up to the plate and DO the things he SAYS he will.

But he doesn't. AND it might be too late now anyway. He says he wants counselling and wants couple's counselling; says he's willing to do what it takes. But he does nothing. I can't wait forever.

I believe I am worth more than waiting on a lie. And, like Andrea says, "Kor, hope is not a strategy".

One thing I am learning is that this self-work is going to be my only way through anything. Putting all else aside – I gotta do this work. I gotta FEEL this pain.

Why would life be so painful? How can the soul be so dark? A Course In Miracles says it's all an illusion, a bad dream – that we are here to remember who we really are. I suppose in order to know something, we must learn its opposite. So in order to learn LOVE we must see, learn and experience the opposite.

The Soul Swamp is like a vast pit of dark gooey swamp water and mud. There's nowhere to go and nothing to do. It's just a big hole of numbing hurtful emotion.

It makes me cry, and almost hyperventilate. I feel so alone and so unbelievably hopeless. I can't tell up from down, right from left. I can only feel an intense amount of sadness and numbness. I don't even know what's next, I don't have any energy to do anything, all I can do right now is stay in my bed in my room, with the blinds closed, and cry.

CHAPTER 21

Seeing with Closed Eyes

2013

IT WAS NOT until I was in therapy that I began to learn the skill of self-observation. Once I did, I was able to start tapping into the vastness of my own human heart—and it took time. Before that, I was vacant; no longer cared if I lived or died. Before that, I was beyond lost, consumed by frustration and numbness.

My life felt like a giant failure. I felt wholly-purposeless.

My therapist, Marcus, had me place my hand on my heart over and over again. I had never truly connected with its rhythmic beat—more than twenty-eight years of dedicated service to my body and mind. So, when I did, all I could do was cry. An infinite number of tears needed to be cried from countless times I'd ignored the very centre of a life-giving force—my own dedicated and unwavering heart.

January 14, 2013

I had counselling on Thursday – once again we spend the whole time talking about 'him'. Marcus went over the importance for me to let go of my anger. When he did, it was like a switch went off in my brain; Marcus is right, the anger is only hurting me. Ultimately, I want to walk from this love I have with 'him' (PH) – he was the first person whom I really loved. I don't want to hate him. For so long I felt so angry that 'I wasn't worth the fight' to him. Angry that he wouldn't go to therapy. 'He' has his own hurts and demons – and like everyone, I am sure he is doing the best job he can with what he knows.

I hope he gets help. I hope that one day he and I can work things out. Right now I know I have a lot of healing to do. I also have a lot of 'creating my own life' to do. I have to work on my faith in the universe. I know some way, somehow, things will work out.

Accept and surrender.

⊷▭◉ ◉▭⊶

January 16, 2013

I am determined to get out of this three year slump I've been in. I need to create an independent life for myself, find my spark, re-learn some self-love, and heal old wounds.

I want to have stability in work and be doing something meaningful. I want to feel happy again. Don't know where my life is going but I do know that I am once again ready to surrender – I am glad I am more able to let go of my anger towards him; I really did and still do love him. We made some mistakes, but he sure has taught me a lot. I hope we work out in the end, but no matter what, I want us to walk away ready for happiness.

I miss Kim a lot.

Work seems to be getting better.

I'm trying hard to let go of him, its hard and I want to text him now, but repeating the old will get the same results. It's time to let go and let things shift – I may lose him, but it's my only option.

⊷▭◉ ◉▭⊶

January 16, 2013 (evening entry)

Counselling was really interesting tonight. The energy in the room was totally different – calm, painful, quiet, dense, healing. Marcus said that I literally look different – softer.

My mother energy was there tonight, she was safe, warm. There was love. She was red velvet. When she was there Little Kori sat on a chair and ate ice cream. Little Kori was content. It made me cry.

⊷▭◉ ◉▭⊶

January 21, 2013

I spent Saturday, in Banff, with him (even though on Friday he drunkenly freaked out on me, again). I went to his son's hockey game (even though I said I didn't want to). I'm not mad or anything, but I don't feel like giving this situation any more of my attention tonight.

→►═◉ ◉═◄←

January 22, 2013

Counselling was good today; it's really the only place I feel fully safe and grounded. Marcus is not mad that I saw 'him' (PH) – he just asks questions, and tells me to stay conscious and aware.

My homework:

- find friends I feel fully safe around
- go back to the gym
- look into school
- stay soft and create a soft atmosphere

I will write more tomorrow, I am exhausted…

→►═◉ ◉═◄←

January 23, 2013

…writing more

Self-focus: Planting and preparing my life's garden.

Strong Women: Kim, Andrea, Emily, Laura, Terry, Elena, Mum, Sally.

Fitness: Yoga, Running, Stairs, Spinning.

Self-growth: School, Reading, Counselling.

Spirit: Meditation, Reading, Prayer.

→►═◉ ◉═◄←

January 28, 2013

Marcus wants me to come up with my counselling topic for tomorrow – there are so many things.

I've had an interesting, conflict filled week with 'him'. He's been mad at me every day. I keep losing focus. I'm not grounded – I am when I journal, but I forget quickly. I forget who I want to become, I forget what I am capable of. The negative voices take over.

Maybe I need to make a visual something I can carry with me – read every day; mantras, words, ideas, thoughts. Maybe my topic should deal with the concept of shame; some of my most intimate surrenders: intimacy, trust, finance.

I was more vulnerable with 'him' (PH) than I was with anyone – he made fun of every aspect of my vulnerability. I can see the person I want to be – so what's getting in the way?

Shame. The belief that I am unworthy; unlovable. I don't want people to know who I am.

SHAME… my secrets… lack of success, not smart, lack of education, failed at running a business, no savings, no real earnings, violence in my relationship, unhealthy life, one night stand at Stampede, sex, I'm not over 'him'.

I deal with shame by withdrawing.

⤜◉ ◉⤛

January 30, 2013

'LETTING GO'

Losing you is as painful as losing my Dad. I don't want to let go. I don't want to say goodbye. I don't want this to die.

You are always mad at me and always holding a grudge from the past; always untruthful, and you keep secrets. It's very unhealthy. I should be able to walk, but I'm stuck.

The thought of losing you is unbearable to me. The thought of being with a jealous, untrusting, controlling man, who lies to me, is also unbearable.

Who has earned the right to hear my story?

‹‹═‹ ›═›‹

February 5, 2013

I have counselling in thirty minutes – I'm not sure what I will bring to the table. I feel like I'm getting stronger, I feel like I am slowly starting to reconnect with myself and remember who I am and what I love.

I still can't shake 'him' (PH). Sometimes never talking to him is all I want. Sometimes 'he' is the only one I want to talk to.

What I really want is to create a life I love. Good and meaningful work. Deep relationships.

Lately, I see men, and I see qualities I want – kind, healthy, driven, free, loving, successful, trusting. Sometimes I question if 'he' will ever be that.

Lately, I am starting to remember that I am interesting and unique and that I am a good catch.

‹‹═‹ ›═›‹

February 6, 2013

Counselling was extremely hard last night. We delved into God and spirituality. I remembered how important prayer and a spiritual practice are for me.

I have been avoiding God – if there is such a thing. Nothing in my life is working out and believing in God isolates me.

To be honest, I think the depth of my spirituality is a complete curse.

It's hard; lonely.

I can't believe how hurt I still am about Dad dying. I can't believe 'God' would take away a brother, a Dad and a Grammy. Then Emily, Kim, and Andrea move. And now I'm expected to let go of 'him'?!?!

He is 'that' person who cares about money and trips, and he lives superficially. Things do not bother him (PH). I have one foot in 'that' and the other in my authentic self – spirit, God, love, humanity.

I know I have to make a choice. I'm sick of hard choices. I'm sick of being lost. I'm sick of losing those I love. I'm sick of fucking praying and getting no response. I'm sick of hurting, falling, failing, and wondering

IS THERE A GOD? WHY DON'T YOU ANSWER ME? I HATE YOU RIGHT NOW

⇥⬤ ⬤⬸

February 9, 2013

Saturday morning – no hangover – waking up alone! Only issue, Friday night was all fighting.

It is becoming clear to me that things will never work with him – he is so controlling, there is no room for me to be me.

Life is too precious and important to be CONSTANTLY fighting and worried about jealous, controlling people who say they care – but don't.

So, God, I need your help. How do I get out of this? I am not a bird meant to be locked in a cage. I don't know how to walk away, it hurts so much.

⇥⬤ ⬤⬸

February 11, 2013

Today is my last day being twenty-eight. Twenty-nine is next. Hard to believe. I hope this year makes sense. I pray I find direction. I pray for peace.

Parts of me are really starting to come to terms with the facts that he and I may never work. I don't know how to walk though. He seems to be putting in an effort.

I just need space. I need space to breathe, to feel, to be myself without having to answer to anyone.

When I sit down and ask myself what I need – the answer is space; alone time. The answer includes no drinking, enjoying healthy food, working out, sprouting (growing sprouts), journaling, tea, cooking, ME time.

→≡○ ○≡←

February 13, 2013

My birthday was amazing! He put in a huge effort.

He delivered flowers, truffle oil, and tea on Monday. On my actual birthday he brought me coffee and gifts and drove me to work. After work we went for wine and listened to live music with my family.

He booked a hotel and a SLEIGH RIDE for Sunday!

Huge effort.

→≡○ ○≡←

February 26, 2013

Where do I even start?

My birthday: 'He' (yes, I am STILL talking to 'him') made the hugest effort – he brought me flowers, arranged for my family to come out for wine, took me to stay in Banff and the Rimrock Hotel, and took me for a sleigh ride.

I really thought he was making an effort. I came home from Banff and emailed my Mum and Marcus!

AND THEN

I catch him in more lies!!

SO I FORGAVE (even though he barely apologized)

AND THEN

Tonight I see all of these emails from August to November from some girl; and he is busy being a TOTAL pervert telling her he wants to stick his dick in her and fuck her all day and "cum" together. Of course I confront him and HE GETS MAD at ME. The difference this time is that I'm much less hooked than I used to be. I'm becoming less and less into this. I'm sick of it, it's almost becoming funny to me at this point. It's so fucked – SO WHY GO BACK??

→▬ ▬←

March 3, 2013

COSTA RICA

Today is day two here in Costa Rica. I have eaten the best pineapple, banana, mango, watermelon, avocado, cucumber, tomato, spinach, and sprouts ever. I'm trying to remain grounded, centred and connected. I'm beginning to believe that maybe the spirit tradition I fit in with is WICCA. I love the earth and the moon. I love remedies and plants. I love humans and community.

I believe in the divine, but I am also scared of it.

I miss him a ton. Authentic? Or just the cycle? I don't know.

I went surfing today. It was so much fun – will probably go again tonight.

Dead God, please send me clear guidance on him. Will this work? Or do I need to let go?

→▬ ▬←

March 15, 2013

The story continues. He showed up in Costa Rica. We had an amazing time. I suggested we give this another try as an exclusive boyfriend/girl-friend for six months—six months with clear boundaries. And, if after six months it is not working, we must walk away, knowing we tried everything.

Maybe it's the worst idea – maybe it's the best – I don't know. I do know that limbo land is not working and it is extremely damaging; so here we go.

⇢▬◉ ◉▬⇠

March 17. 2013

He and I wrote out some boundaries, and will be in touch with a counsellor this week – I have hope – at least this will help us move on or close the chapter -

I will be diligent about my growth.

I will be diligent about my growth.

I will be diligent about my growth.

I will be diligent

I will be

I will

I

CHAPTER 22

Significant Six — Progress

2013

THREE DAYS AFTER PH and I wrote up some boundaries, because we'd agreed to give 'us' another try—a six months exclusive relationship to make it work or walk away—I wrote a letter to Marcus, my therapist, Marcus.

Six was significant; six months previous I'd first sat in front of Marcus to begin my healing journey.

March 20, 2013

Marcus, I'm journaling… and crying… and writing… and I just wanted to share with you where I am at.

The biggest thing I am learning in counselling is self-compassion and self-love. I have learned to slow down. I have started to take care of myself in the deepest way I know how. I have stopped asking the people I look up to 'am I normal?', 'is this the right path?' and I have started to accept that there is no 'normal' and there is no final goal. Life is NOW. I have learned that no matter how badly I want to get through a lesson and be done with it, sometimes life has a different plan, and sometimes it is more about the journey than the destination.

I, for the first time in my life am learning to be SOFT and VULNERABLE. I am also learning that softness is actually really strong, and really beautiful. I have never acknowledged the power and strength in soft, feminine, open energy, instead I lived from a place of hard, masculine energy which I used to purposefully self-protect. Now I see that, for me, wisdom can be accessed when I am soft, tearful, vulnerable, open, self-compassionate, and real with where my heart is at.

I am learning to be seen, authentically and deeply seen. And I am learning to show up, not in a hard and self-protected way, but in a 'heart inside out and totally vulnerable to the harshness of life' kind of way. I'm proud of that, even though it scares the fuck out of me and makes me cry. I'm learning to love being soft.

I have learned that losing Dad hurt me and traumatized me more than I ever realized. I'm learning to develop a relationship with Little Kori; it hurt me so much, six months ago, when I met her and she would not talk to me. She still won't talk to me, but we're developing some trust, and I know it will take time. I am learning that I avoid 'hurt' with an energy-filled angry story, but if I stop, slow down, and breathe, then, almost all of the time I take that action, I am able to touch my hurting heart. I am learning that 'hurt' is ok, and that it must be felt and moved through - you cannot ignore it or skip over it.

I am learning that I have felt profoundly alone for the majority of my existence. That hurts me beyond words. I am also learning that through a relationship with God, and a relationship with myself, I will be able to start to fill those holes and take care of me. I also have learned that I have an endless troop of personalities to keep me company :)

I am learning that a relationship with God (or whatever I will decide to call that 'power' when I figure it out) is key to my 'life garden'. I have learned that in order for me to be balanced I need: gratitude, prayer (for me and for the world), deep connection (with people and life), purposeful work, strong female relationships, self-growth, counselling, earth foods, good wine, and physical activity. I have learned in this process that holding the space to plant my garden with all the right soil is mandatory for my purpose on this planet. I have learned that I love witches, and fairies, and gardening, and sprouting!

I am slowly starting to trust life again... slowly. I am deeply grateful for the 'soul swamp' I have been swimming in. Because no matter how helpless, dark, or alone I've felt, being in the soul swamp shows me contrast.

I have learned that I want a life with a successful business, children, and a loving partner. I long to love and be loved more than anything else. I am learning that I deeply want a loving, committed, trusting, playful, free relationship in which I can be who I am, and BE SEEN by my partner. I want to be strong and yet retain a vulnerability of sorts—a softness. I want a deep connection, and I want to be let into my partner's world as well. I want to be valued and recognized. I want to have a family and to make this world a better place.

My whole theory in life has always been 'self-love' but Love', but this process has made me understand that 'self-love' is more than two words, and more than an affirmation. Self-love is a place that is reached through a dark and painful journey into the depths of the soul, for through that route there is the true light. The concept makes me weep because of its profundity.

Marcus, thank you for all your help so far. I'm so frigging scared for the next steps.

Chapter 23

Optimistic Tones

2013

April 1, 2013

I'm glad that I chose to do counselling. And I'm glad we are taking additional counselling for couples.

'He' and I have started the process of going to couples counselling. It seems good. It was just that the assessment…

… well… I'm nervous. I take this kind of thing seriously and am committed to the work it will take – I fear that he won't make the time for homework. I'm scared that I will never learn to trust – he has told me so many lies.

I hope it all works out. I need to stay focused and diligent on my work – self-love, self-care, and self-compassion.

~~⬥~~

April 9, 2013

I'm loving working for INLIV, running the wellness office at Canadian Natural Resources Limited (CNRL). I'm loving coaching – makes me feel like my day has meaning.

My interview for the Canadian School of Natural Nutrition (CSNN), to determine whether I can attend as a student, is on Thursday. I am really excited.

Things with 'him' and 'me' are going well, he is very open and receptive to our homework and the reading we've been asked to do. I'm learning a lot about men and women, and I'm learning a lot about how I am in relationships. This will be worth the process, no matter what.

--⟫⊜ ⊜⟪--

April 10, 2013

A year ago I had no idea what was coming for me; it's weird driving home from bootcamp these days with the nice(ish) weather and the long days. SO MUCH has happened and changed for me. I have entered the most painful parts of my inner world – I have experienced indescribable heartbreak – I have also been blessed to learn about unconditional love, and fortunate to experience amazing friendships. I have finally started to process Dad dying and how MUCH it hurt me. Life is different... and the same.

God and Dad, I love you. Thank you.

Please give me strength and wisdom. Please help me make the best choices for my life – even if they are hard. Is he right for me?

--⟫⊜ ⊜⟪--

April 15, 2013

On Thursday I had my interview at CSNN. And I GOT IN!!!

Kim came and visited on the weekend (which was amazing). I've missed her so much.

I feel out of balance today – I spent so many days with him, and NONE with myself and none with friends.

I cannot lose myself.

--⟫⊜ ⊜⟪--

April 18, 2013

What I am scared of the most right now is losing what I have worked so hard for in counselling. I don't want to ever, ever feel how I did a year ago. I want to keep working on being SOFT, OPEN, VULNERABLE. I'm used to being so closed off, distant, and hard.

I'm scared to lose myself.

Dad and God – please help!

How do I remain soft, open, feminine?

My self-work has to remain my priority.

I have to stay focused, grounded, and present in order to show up in my own life.

→▭ ◁▭◁

April 29, 2013

Shit hit the fan this weekend

He decided to verbally attack me in the bar on Friday. I am becoming extremely resentful toward him that I am working my ass off at self-growth, and working hard at managing my feelings and emotions through this process, and he is not doing the same.

I did, however, lose control on Friday and I physically lashed out at him. Pushing him, and pinching him on his arms and legs. I freaked out and scratched the hell out of my arm – it's bandaged right now, the cut measures two-inches square – worst pain.

I begged him again, yelled at him, physically freaked out. And afterwards I became calm. Then I freaked out again. Basically I was trying to manage myself.

He told me that I put no effort in, that he is sick of chasing me around, that I am fucked up and unfixable. He told me that I am a bully to the couples therapist. He told me he didn't care, and wasn't sure he wanted me anymore. He told me I should no longer hang out with Emily. He demanded answers (as to where I was) from our time apart (he doesn't give me ANY answers, and EVERYTHING I know is because I found out myself, from snooping).

It's a double standard.

He is back to completely ignoring what I say. I had such hope on Friday after counselling, and now I have less hope and a very broken heart. It is so hard for me to trust this…'him'… and this is why:

I have shared my most intimate details about counselling with him – and he throws them in my face. Told me that I will fuck every relationship up that I am in. He told me he is sick of me being selfish and he thinks I always have issues - told me he does not want to hear about counselling anymore.

I just don't know what to think. I need to focus on ME again. I will continue to be selfish in this process because I am becoming a better person. If he does not like that, then we will each have to move on and find someone new.

I would miss him if he chose that. But I will not regress and, this is too important.

⋅→▤ ▤←⋅

I bounced back and forth. Part of me could see that this was incredibly unhealthy, and the other part seemed to only feel at peace when I was with PH.

In hindsight, I understand that each person has to process his or her own journey within an abusive relationship.

Dear Reader:

To hold back journal entries from you would not illustrate the amount of 'back and forth' involved in my story. To feature only some journal entries would not example the long-term-ness of 'textbook' dysfunction.

We take a risk when we share our stories in print. Is the content balanced? Will I connect with the reader? Will each reader hear me? Will each reader hear herself in me? But the most important thing is, when sharing about abuse, is to document, even when it seems repetitive, for it is in those repetitions—those 'same shit, different day' entries—that each can identify herself, recognize similarities, spot patterns, and then relate events to her own journey.

And it is through that connection, that healing can begin to take place; knowing you are not the only one who has experienced, is experiencing, has survived, is surviving, has moved through, can move through the darkness.

CHAPTER 24

Truths Emerge

2013

May 6, 2013

I'm starting to feel more in touch with myself than I have in years. I think living a healthy life means becoming clear about one's identity. That in taking care of yourself, you are becoming stronger and feel validated.

I'm learning to touch-in with my heart and ask: "What do I need?"

I'm trying to develop my inner 'Oprah energy' – that part of me that is so internally connected, self-aware, and self-loving.

Things were really, really great until the past two weekends. He's demonstrating old, controlling behaviors. He does not seem interested in doing the work required. Part of me is not sure it's going to work. I'm scared to lose him, but I am not willing to give up what I know I need to be happy.

Two weekends ago he called me 'fucked up' and 'unfixable'. This weekend he told me that I 'do not act like a girlfriend'. He does not think I should be friends with 'people like Emily'.

A part of me loves that we are so different, and other parts of me want a man who is into self-growth and development. I want someone who will dance with me when we go out. Someone goofy. Someone who does not drink so much.

The work on 'us' is still new. I need to have patience.

God, I pray for clarity, connection, and strength.

⇀═◎ ◎═↼

May 12, 2013

Hard weekend in counselling with him; I'm beginning to have doubts.

God, are you around? Sometimes I feel so lost and so alone. Sometimes I feel like everything is such an upstream battle.

I miss you Dad. I wish I could just have one visit with you. Why did you leave me?

⋅→▭ ◑▭←⋅

May 13, 2013

I'm really craving a cute condo that I could live in on my own. A one-bedroom loft downtown would be perfect.

I'm missing Emily, Kim, travel, and festivals. I miss running.

What is it that I need?

⋅→▭ ◑▭←⋅

May 15, 2013

No matter how hard life can be – GIRLFRIENDS help!

I would love to live on a commune and have an amazing wellness centre. I want to rent or own my own cute condo and decorate it in a really feminine and soft style.

I want freedom in a relationship to fully, one-hundred-percent, be me – no jealousy, no control.

Clear Shadow, aka: Ursula, What are you showing me? I welcome you and your lessons.

⋅→▭ ◑▭←⋅

May 28, 2013

I saw Marcus, the therapist, today. This week my focus is 'hand to heart', a real focus on self-connection.

Looking back on my journal and my life in the past year, I really feel like I have come a long way.

Today when I touch my heart, I feel alone and content. I feel fluttery, like I am divinely connected.

I'm learning self-love and self-compassion – I'm learning to take care of myself.

Once again, I believe in God.

⤙▬ ▬⤚

May 29, 2013

Truth: I'm scared. I'm scared of life. Scared to grow. I'm scared to keep hurting and feeling so alone. I'm scared to keep having to stand in truth and risk losing friends and family. Why do I feel so alone all of the time?

May 30, 2013

Patience, Kori!

⤙▬ ▬⤚

June 5, 2013

He and I went for a few beers again yesterday, and two turned into too many (again), and then we got into a physical fight. What the FUCK is wrong with us?

Parts of my life are starting to work well. Other parts (like drinking) are not working at all!

Maybe I have a drinking problem?

I don't know if he and I are going to work and that makes me extremely nervous. I feel so all alone.

⤙▬ ▬⤚

Kori Hagel

June 6, 2013

I feel very low energy today. I stayed home from work. We have counselling with a new therapist tonight and I'm extremely nervous – don't know if I'll mention the physical violence – I'm embarrassed.

June 6, 2013 (later in the day)

We went to see a new therapist and I feel a little more hopeful. He seems like a really straightforward counsellor. We will see.

I'm just not sure that 'he' and I are meant to be together, I'm beginning to wonder if we are really different people. I'll always love him, but I'm not sure (about us and our future) right now.

July 17, 2013

I saw Marcus last night, my biggest learning is (A) how 100% diligent and dedicated I have to be to process, because if I'm not, I quickly disconnect, (B) how sneaky disconnection is.

For me, disconnection happens when I am not dedicated to my practice.

My lease ends in less than a month. I had planned to live on my own, but I have been unable to find a place. I am going to live with 'him' and make a home, and if it does not work I will simply find a new place.

God I need help and guidance. Please help me remain awake and please guide me.

July 24, 2013

Why do I resist journaling?

I believe that being a 'human' on earth is temporary… I'm just wondering what the fuck my path is? Internally I feel like a witch/healer. I

100

get excited about music, drums, costumes, food, healing, fairies, dancing... and then I disconnect from it all – almost too easily. I'm not sure
how to stay with that energy. I wish I could grow flowers, be a bee keep-
er, heal people with energy and food. I wish I could travel the world. I'd
like to live somewhere green, wet, and lush.

He's not like that at all. I have a hard time remaining centred around
him. I feel like he is always keeping secrets from me. I feel like I lose
track and I do not do the things I need to do to be balanced - like see
my girlfriends. At the same time though, I do love him, and things are
much better (even though I caught him watching porn again).

This entire journal has been about him.

WHAT IS THE LESSON?

KORI - journaling grounds you - do it every day.

Witch: herbs, foods, Mother nature, magic, forest.

Goddess: religion, spirit, eternity, chakras, heaven.

GOD I NEED YOU. I DON'T KNOW MY PATH OR
DIRECTION

Women, Healing, Growth, Magic, Mother Nature.

→─▬◉ ◉▬─←

July 20, 2013

Why is the process of journaling such a difficult thing to commit
to?

There is a lot going on in my head and a lot in life. Where to even
start?

My last therapy session was really hard, we went a lot inward.

It's so strange to connect with myself - this whole process has been
a huge learning curve. A week ago my vision was, once again, so sad.
My heart and the picture in my mind's eye was so dark. It was like: there
I was - a tiny speck all alone in the huge vast and never ending world. It
was a lot like what I used to think heaven was like - a pointless, never-
ending, eternal walk through a long grey tunnel.

It took me a while to push past the sludge to even see my heart. As soon as I did, I just bawled. The deepest most eternal parts of myself feel so unbearably all ALONE. I have always felt this way - it's almost impossible to face it. Even when people are near, I really feel like I'm here on this planet, alone, with no one to truly relate to. I don't know my path. I seem unable to let people in. I just feel different.

Moving in with him is sure bringing out the crazy in me. I'm indescribably scared to be in this, and I'm deeply trying to stay present. It's difficult to manage. I feel like a shitty girlfriend. I'm scared to lose myself, scared to love, and scared for history to repeat.

Marcus pointed out that my job is to stay connected to myself, put me at the centre of my life and work on healing.

On Friday, my friend, Kels, said that we need to be sure as individuals that we have glorious and fulfilling lives, and we fit our partners into that – it's not about giving ourselves away to be with someone, it's about remaining full and balanced and self-loving and creating a life together.

⊷⊨◉ ◉⊨⊶

October 7, 2013

I have been living at his house for eight weeks, and so far it's awful. TONS of fighting. This weekend has been a total run-away and I'm extremely disappointed in myself. I don't think 'we' are going to work out.

Later the same day (October 7, 2013)

I'm so mad at myself for how this weekend went. I drank so much booze, snorted coke, and had zero water. I ate nothing on Saturday except some eggs benny. I haven't done this in a while – it's unacceptable.

I have therapy tomorrow and, strangely enough, I am excited.

Here are my true thoughts. I don't think he and I are going to win at this. That makes me mad. And I am scared to death. I'm hurting. I wanted this SO MUCH. He's refusing to go to therapy – I really don't know how to fix it all. I don't want to walk away, but I'm not happy and neither is he.

Since I moved into his condo, I feel like I'm in a constant energy battle. A war of energy. He hates hearing me talk about therapy, girlfriends, school, work, spirituality. The thing is, those are the things I am interested in—all those things I hope, dream, and feel passion for are important to me. They are part of me. He told me I am not interesting. It hurts. I really love him, but I cannot sacrifice internal love to make this work.

I am SO GRATEFUL for school. I love it. I'm so grateful for therapy. I'm glad Emily is home, and I am so glad I have Kim. I'm glad I have a relationship with God again

⋯⟞◉ ◉⟝⋯

November 7, 2013

Dear God,

I hate you sometimes. Why the fuck doesn't anything ever work???? I show up to you, I show up to life, I am a good person, I try hard.... And THIS.

Job, money, relationships, independence, education... why won't ANYTHING work?

I have been trying HARD. So hard. I have walked a courageous path. I have stood by my word. I have supported others. I have been dedicated to growth and evolution. WHY WON'T YOU HELP ME??????

You take my Brother. You take my Dad. You left my Mum with four children (how could you do that?) You put me through so much shit as a kid and a teenager. You give me a boyfriend/partner—him—the not so charming Prince. You make me love him. You make it impossible to leave him. I have no money. You give me some fucking passion that is not something I can make a damn living from. WHY?????

What the fuck do you want from me??? WHAT IS IT???? WHAT. DO. YOU. WANT. FROM. ME???

Is life just simply supposed to suck? Are you some kind of invention made up by some pathetic people who could not bear the shitty circumstances of life? Is this whole thing a joke??? I don't get it.

I am trying hard here. I am trying hard to find a reason. To follow a path. To believe in YOU... so where the fuck are you??? How long are you going to watch me struggle?

Angels? Divine intervention??? YEAH, FUCKING RIGHT. What the hell???

I don't care if I don't fall in love. I don't care if I don't have kids. I don't care if I'm alone forever...

... but it would be really NICE if SOMETHING could work.

⇥◉ ◉⇤

Nov 13, 2013

Dear God.

I do not understand you or this life. I feel so afraid to let go and so afraid to hold on.

I know that our thoughts create our reality. I know that there is an infinite and divine power that runs this whole operation. I know in my heart that the same force that has the sun come up each morning, that has the stars internally sparkle and that has a sperm meet an egg and magically turn into a human is the same force that governs my life.

But why am I having such a hard time believing (that magic) it is accessible to me?

Why is everything a struggle?

Why can't I figure out a path?

Why is money such a huge issue for me?

How come some people have such abundance?

What happened to me?

I used to FIRMLY believe all of this (magic and trust in life). But looking back, it didn't matter how firmly I believed it – it still didn't work out. Why? Truly what am I doing wrong?

I wish I knew what the plan was. I wish I could at least trust that there is a plan for me.

Why can't I let go of him? Or be with him? Why can't I make money? Why is everything an upstream battle? What am I doing wrong?

My dialogue is so negative. What do I do to switch it? Will switching it even work?

Dear inner witch. What would you do?

(WITCH) Kori, I think I would move to California. Or at least go and visit there, alone, without him. Rent a car, pack a bag and go do some yoga and drink some juice. There is something waiting for you there. It does not mean that you will live there, move there, own a business there. It is beyond what you think could happen.

(KORI) I don't know, Witch. I think this is just my friend Dean's idea. Not mine. I think it might be the power of suggestion, implanted in my mind and growing like a weed.

(WITCH) Weeds have a lot of purpose and nutritional value Kori. You are even getting one tattooed on your back.

(KORI) What the fuck kind of advice is that? Seriously?

(WITCH) You need to wake up. Stay awake and start following your gut, your intuition. Stop being so scared, you never know what is waiting for you in your life. Book a ticket – go and have some fun. And leave this coffee shop. This is silly to sit here and be mad at the internet. Maybe you should go and visit your Dad's grave. Write down the directions. I think the internet will work to sign on and find out the directions.

Note: I'd been in a coffee shop that I often frequented. The internet always worked there. But it wasn't working that day. I used my computer for some automatic writing, to gain wisdom from the great void. This time I'd talked to my inner witch. I was humbled by her wisdom. When I finished talking to her, the internet signal returned. I got the directions to my Dad's grave, then left the coffee shop. I spent the afternoon crying beside his tombstone.

Mid-November, 2013.

I'm 29. I live at my parent's home. I behave as if I hate my family. I have no job security. I'm unhappy living in this stupid city. I spend my time thinking that maybe this is all because of my thoughts… so I try to be positive. I read books, I go to therapy, I help people, I meditate, I visualize letting go… letting go of the things that no longer serve me… I exercise, (God) I respect your planet, I stand up for people with no voice… When the FUCK are YOU going to SHOW up???

CHAPTER 25

Expansion
2013

ONE OF MY favourite teachers at nutrition school was Dr. Joe, a Naturopathic Doctor. He was one of the smartest people I had ever met. For some reason I was always able to really open up to him. I felt drawn to tell him things I would usually only tell my therapist—strange, since I did not have a lot of trust in men. I found it interesting to watch my heart begin to trust.

On **November 22, 2013**, I sent an email to Dr. Joe

Dear Dr. Joe,

So, first of all I am just going to say something - exactly how I feel it. I really look up to you. I feel like you're my mentor, and it's crazy because I have never had someone that I want to 'be just like when I grow up.'

So, I will leave most of my thoughts for my journal, but when I came home I just sat down on the floor and cried. Unexpected, I know. This is what I learned from a colon hydrotherapy session… again …unexpected.

Letting Go. Trusting the Process. That's what really stood out for me today. I wanted to cry so bad when I was there, talking about my Dad. But I didn't.

I actually trust you, for some unknown reason, and its odd to me because I don't think I trust a lot of people; not deep trust.

I'm not letting go. I can see that in not letting go of 'him' (the long term abusive boyfriend/partner), not letting go of my Dad, not letting go of anger, and not letting go in colon hydrotherapy, that I'm not trusting life. I'm not trusting people.

You have helped strengthen my desire to help women.

Enough thoughts from me.

Thanks. As always, the universe has thrown me on a path that is scaring the shit out of me and also LIGHTING ME UP SO MUCH!

November 26, 2013

Dear Dr. Joe,

I feel worse than I have in weeks. I'm so moody (it's not physically manifesting, it's just bubbling in me), and I'm deeply angry, and sad, and I'm pretty much totally constipated. Is this still from my week of eating like a maniac? Or is this all part of the colon hydrotherapy cleansing process?

Everything about my diet is the same as usual. I'm managing my stress with meditation, therapy, writing, seeing friends, and breathing. My exercise has been less because I feel too drained of positive energy to do a hard-core gym workout (those workouts just infuriate me right now, which has NEVER been the case with hard-core workouts; I usually love them).

I hope your exam was amazing!

I turned last week's learning into a blog post for the INLIV newsletter – it's titled 'Letting Go - Unexpected Lessons on the Hydro Colon Therapy Table'. Haha, it will freak people out, but they will be too curious NOT to read it!

Response from Dr. Joe

It would be unusual for the colon therapy to leave you feeling more constipated. It may sometimes leave you without a BM for a couple days as there is little stool in the bowel, but not to feel all plugged up.

Take some coconut oil, maybe 1 tablespoon a day, to lubricate. And take a couple of tablespoons of ground flaxseed. Keep up the hydration. Releasing anger often looks like this. Grief hits women in the gut; whereas in men it is more liver.

I am confident it will all "work its way out" in due time. Your brain activity can really have an effect on all this as well.

Blast through a workout anyhow and see if that gets the ball rolling.

Thanks for asking about the exam. It was REALLY hard. I did manage to stay within the time limits and get everything done. The oral part of it was stressful and almost overwhelming, but I do feel I conquered it! Some other candidates looked like they had seen a ghost.

See you Friday.

INLIV ARTICLE

Letting Go – The Unexpected Lessons On The Hydro Colon Therapy Table.

I had a bizarre and unexpected reaction to my session on this past Friday. I came home, sat down on the floor, and cried uncontrollably. I'm talking serious sobbing; a total emotional release. Odd right? That was not on the list of possible side effects, but I think it should be. I couldn't tell you why this happened, but I'm going to try anyway.

While on the table I was having a hard time 'releasing'. I apologize for the unpleasant details, but this is important! Bowel movements are important; period. They give such insight into the state of your health.

Our physical state is a direct manifestation of our emotional state. So a hard time releasing spoke absolute volumes to me about my ability in life to 'let go'. My heart was so heavy when I came home, I couldn't help but cry. What am I holding onto? Why am I holding on? What is so hard about 'letting go'?

It's truly amazing to me what cleansing brings up. When we cleanse, there is no doubt that we cleanse physical toxins in our bodies, but what I tell my clients before they cleanse is to be aware and prepared that, through a cleanse, you are also cleansing your emotional body. We carry thoughts, ideas and beliefs that are toxic. Cleansing always bring them up and puts them smack down in front of us to look at.

Letting go is really, really hard. Letting go, trusting life, being open and vulnerable, it's a challenge; a deep soul challenge. When we are able to let go and be vulnerable, we are open to love, healing, and new possibility. So why then, is letting go so hard?

Perhaps we get stuck in the familiar. We get lost in the mental chatter that all too often speaks to us in a negative manner. Maybe we feel defeated. We may feel that the Universe has been unjust, and our hearts may be broken. That's a hard thing to bounce back from and to let go of.

Louise Hay, a hero of mine, affirms: "It is safe for me to let go", which makes me keenly aware that in order to let go we must truly believe it is safe to do so. We have to trust the process.

Suddenly 'letting go' gets even deeper.

Do you trust the process? Is it safe for you to let go of the things that no longer serve you? Maybe it's a job, or an unhealthy relationship, or extra weight. Whatever it is, ask yourself this: "Is it safe for me to let go"? Your answer will give you direction of where to go and what to do.

Letting go not only requires trust, but it needs a good dose of courage. Courage is at the core of who we are. We are made of courage, sometimes we forget that, but I am here to remind you that your very essence is courage. Courage means stepping into the land of the unknown, which puts us in the path of total vulnerability.

Deepak Chopra put it into words I love: "Are you willing to welcome uncertainty?" Brilliant.

So what's it going to take for you to look deep within, to ask yourself what is no longer serving you and to courageously let it go, trusting that you are destined for truly fabulous things. Your life matters. Yes, you, the one reading this. You matter. You are worth every breath you take.

And that, my friends, is what I took away from a one hour Hydro Colon Therapy session.

CHAPTER 26

The More Progress, The More Fear

2013

November 23, 2013.

    I want to own a business. The dream won't go away. I need help.

I'D HAD MY fair share of madness. But I suppose there was a particular period of time where my madness was rather unmanaged and became intensely loud.

"When it comes to art, it's important not to hide the madness"

Herodes Atticus

When I'd moved out of 'his' house… again… I moved back with my parents.

No adult child should live with his or her parents.

The first year of therapy isolated me, cushioned me somewhat, in a slow, somber depression. Lots of tears on my own. A lot of long baths, followed by early nights in bed. There was simply so much to process.

The second year allowed me to process extreme anger. Different than the first stage of emotional detox, I had to face my fury.

I remember feeling the rage daily, it was like a fire at my base chakra—as if anger bubbled up from my vagina. I didn't know what that meant, but it was there, and it was alive, confusing, and uncomfortable. I just wanted to crawl out of my skin and run the hell away.

The timing of my move couldn't have been worse. My parents had just returned from their second home in Costa Rica. Dad had Dengue fever, and Mum was recovering from it. Apparently, she almost died in Costa Rica that year; she had been so dehydrated she almost went into renal failure.

Though it was frightening and shocking to hear that, it stirred my anger. I was so pissed off that she hadn't taken care of herself.

I remembered my time in Australia, when Mum (missing me) had emailed and said if I didn't come home it would be like she was losing her second child. I realize now, she meant it in a 'loving me, missing me' way, but it stung. I can't imagine what it was like for her to lose my older brother to such tragedy. Neither can I place myself in her shoes: a Mother whose daughter was falling in love with another country, and who was in a relationship with a man on that other continent. My Mum and I were so close when I was growing up my time away in Australia and New Zealand was difficult for her.

But when she went to Costa Rica, it was my turn to have a difficult time with her absence. And difficult, for me, meant pissed off. Righteous indignation, my uncle called it. Being angry only hurts the self—no one else.

So there I was in my parent's house, basically and wholly fucking pissed off. I was ticked that my relationship failed. I was exasperated because my skin itched with rage—I so hated being trapped in my own body that it broke out in hives, became constipated, raged to the point of self-harming, experienced insomnia, depression, and anxiety. And, as my physical body betrayed me, I raged on.

I was angry with myself because the only solution I could come up with was to go and live with my parents.

To say I was a difficult houseguest would be an understatement. My anger with myself manifested as fury toward them. I judged their relationship, their individuality, their choices, their experiences so harshly from the point of rage that was wholly my own.

At the time I was moving through a bout of terrible insomnia; months without proper sleep. And, even at my healthiest, I am sensitive to sound and I need complete quiet for sleep—the noise from a murmuring television, or even low conversation is enough to trigger insomnia and anger.

I was at a point in my life where I was hypersensitive. The complications in my life had driven me to the edge. It was like in the movie *Train Watchers,* where the main character is detoxing from heroin, and the audio and cinematography captures all the sound in an exaggerated and nerve-hitting style. The sounds of the clocks, the buzz of the lights, the murmur of television, the conversation between people, the traffic of the city—it all drove me crazy.

So unreasonable was I that, one night, I got out of bed, opened the door and screamed, "Would you shut the fuck up? I AM TRYING TO SLEEP!" This was directed at both parents, my Brothers, and a family friend. Teenage style temper tantrums from a 29 year old daughter/guest of the house were clearly not welcome. It did not go over well.

I don't think my parents knew what to do with me. Fair enough, I know *I* had no idea what to do with my own self. My sanity was slipping, and fast.

School was my safe haven at the time. I loved being there. It was an escape from the demented reality in which I was living, but more than that, it was a place that I felt seen and understood. I thrived inside the classroom. I excelled at the subjects.

Each night, after class, I would get into my car and break down in tears of gratitude.

I was so proud of myself for taking that course.

I had a yearning to devour the curriculum, but no big picture as to how I might apply it. It was a kind of blind and absolute faith that this was my path.

It was the first healthy decision in years, perhaps ever, that I'd made on my own. I had not asked for advice or approval from anyone on this choice, nor did I request financial support.

I had found the course. I had signed up. And I showed up. It was glorious.

At the time I was working as a trainer, personal trainer, and nutritionist. I was paying a lot, each month, for therapy I really had no idea how I'd pay for Holistic Nutrition School. It was a significant amount. But somehow I did it. It was important to me and I was incredibly proud of myself for taking the leap.

I was a broken-winged bird, working on flight.

My truths at that time were too humiliating to share with most people. My truths worried them.

So, outside of the joy of school, thrill of learning, and success at work, there was still an inner demon—that vine. I had gotten into the habit of scratching myself as a coping technique. Though I didn't know why I did it, I presumed it was similar to why cutters cut. I didn't just scratch myself lightly as in 'everyday itching'. I gouged my skin to the point of bleeding and scarring. In hindsight, it was 'gouging' not 'scratching'.

It became quite frequent and it felt good. There was one particular time that it happened in the middle of the night during a rage-induced bout of insomnia. I used my hands, then planted my nails firmly into the skin of my chin and dug deep, wounding myself in pathways from my neck all the way to my collar bone.

I looked as if I'd been attacked by a wild animal.

Neck scratches were hard to cover. Usually when this behaviour occurred I'd be in a zombie state—never fully recalling it until a burning pain woke me in the morning, alerting me something was wrong.

One night after I'd gouged my neck, I went to Earls' restaurant to meet Kim. She'd just come into town.

Kim was never fooled by stories—like 'whoops, I got carried away playing with the dog'. I'm sure, that day, everyone could see the scratches, but not many people would confront another human about an injury so strange, would they?

That night, when Kim asked me what was going on, I told her that I did this to myself. Of course she asked me why. But I had no response. She cried; I don't blame her. I didn't know what was going on either; I was scared too.

That night I stayed out all night and I drank far too much wine. What was a fun and in control night for some was numbing for me. I was out of control and in so much pain.

As much as I loved attending the Canadian School of Natural Nutrition, there remained out of classroom issues, living with my family issues and, in general, still serious inside-Kori issues.

After I'd cried my tears of gratitude, following class, I had to drive about 20 minutes to my parents' home. This took me on the Deerfoot Trail, with the well-known river crossing called the Calf Robe Bridge.

Each time I crossed it, in those months I lived with my parent's, I'd experience massive fear of the self-destructive variety. An urge to drive off it would surface in my core. So strong was the feeling, I had to consciously resist pulling the steering wheel to one side. It would have been so easy: 110 kilometres an hour and an inevitable, cold death. I could do it, with no one to talk me out of it, no one to explain anything to; a dramatic statement as if to say 'fuck you life, fuck you and your stupid lessons.'

The feelings that followed the urge to drive off the bridge were those of shame. Perhaps they were for not carrying out the action, or maybe simply for having initiated the idea that it 'could' be carried out. Either way, I swallowed that disgrace and let it eat away at me.

I had a lot of weird impulses in those days, and I never knew if the part of me that believed that I should die would wind up taking over and just do it.

Before I moved out of 'his' condo we were living on the eleventh floor—it might have been the sixth, though; funny how one can block memories that one swore one would never forget—anyway, it was high enough that any sane human would never consider jumping from.

I have never in my life understood the desire to end life via jumping off of a building. To me that choice is downright dramatic and scary. But in those days, with those urges, I stood at the balcony numerous times envisioning the jump. At those times there was a great pull within me to climb the railing and dive off the side of the building. I never told a soul this, I didn't know how to tell anyone about it—I was too paralyzed by shame.

I resisted frightening impulses on a daily basis. I never knew what side of me would prevail. But in absolute honesty—as I now have no other way to operate, I don't lie any more—at that time, it didn't matter what side won. Though I was desperately afraid of what I was capable of, I didn't trust that anything was going to get better. I believe I romanticized death.

CHAPTER 27

Contemplation
2013

As THE END of 2013 approached, I thought about my intense inward journey. Though I'd always been involved in self-discovery—some might say 'self-evolution' is my greatest passion—the recent past comprised a different sort of development: darker—no vision boards, angels, light-energy, or spiritual books—the past sixteen months had been a discovery of darkness.

At first, the darkness robbed me of my energy, and scared me. It enveloped my heart, my soul, my mind, my life. I lived it, I breathed it, I tried to run from it, but its grasp was so all encompassing that the only choice I had was to surrender.

I had to trust that, in the surrender, I'd grow by feeling the contours within myself. I had to allow myself to develop as a seed does when it's planted in the earth. And I had to believe there would come a time when I would not only emerge and feel the difference between the dark inside the earth and the thick velvet black of a moonless sky above the earth, but know that I needed both in order to thrive.

The Kori I'd become had lost her voice, her power, her passion. She had no confidence, no self-love, and no 'spark'. She was depressed, suicidal, and void of all life force. I don't even know how she managed but, if I were to guess, I would say that it was the unconditional love of her best friends, family, and an all forgiving and supportive universe which I refer to as God.

You see, looking back to my 'even younger than now self' I can recall certain times, many times, sometimes all the times, as vividly as if 'those times' had just happened moments ago. Times when I declared I no longer needed God. A time I decided I was sick of his bullshit. Exhausted over nothing ever working out.

I'd told God, 'Thanks, but no thanks. I'm fine on my own.'

Not long after that breakup with God, I'd met the man, PH, with whom I'd spend the years losing myself, forgetting who I was, struggling to be whole.

The more I pushed to be with that man, and begged him to love me, the less I knew myself and loved myself. And the less I loved myself, the more I needed him to compensate.

Toxic. Yes. Acidic. Yes. I never thought I would be 'that girl'.

The positive, driven, spiritual, inspiring, loving, courageous, quirky, filled with faith individual had disappeared. With every self-betrayal, every hangover, every total disregard for her intuition, she became less visible. She would sink deeper and deeper into a numb and disconnected state, only to wake up one day with a broken heart and an overwhelming desire to die.

My heart ached for the person I used to be; or was meant to be.

And, as I grew, through therapy, I remembered that when I'd first moved in with my earth angel, Kim—the women who taught me what unconditional love meant—I'd spent three months having panic attacks, experiencing nightmares, and was rendered almost unable to function. Waking up was the worst part of my day because I would realize my reality. Even though I was hurt and scared and knew in my heart that the break up was the best thing, I missed PH.

No matter what names he called me, no matter how many pictures he texted me of faked-breasted girls he was dating, I missed him. I missed him so much.

Back then, all I could do was cry, drink wine, then sneak out and see him. It took four months of unhealthy weight loss, unable to let go of him, unable to make it through a day without crying, then Kim had insisted that I see someone.

Kim the earth angel moved me forward at a point when I had no fight left in me. She knew that I needed serious help.

I had been embarrassed, humiliated, and shamed. I had had no idea how I'd become so lost. I didn't think I would ever find my passion again. I had no money, no direction, no job, nothing. Absolutely nothing. I gave it all up.

Numbness, for me, was a way of coping with the pain. I disassociated. And that was a way of not facing an issue so large I had no clue where to start. I didn't have the know-how to fix it all. I didn't have the desire.

I'd sold my soul to an ambivalent grief.

No one understood me at the time. No one could understand how Kori Leigh, the self-assured girl, could let this happen. And I had no answer.

And, after months and months and months, when my family was in Costa Rica, (I didn't want to go, I didn't have the money, nor did I have the will, I wanted to be alone) I began enjoying pieces of life, living with my Sister and working at a job I loved. I was excelling in the sport of running. And I worked my therapy program weekly. I was also dipping deep into emotional processing and discovering some intensely wounded parts of my own psyche from which I could no longer run. Learning about boundaries turned my life upside down. I existed in the darkness but, at least at times, I was present in that darkness.

I'd lasted six weeks earlier in the year without seeing or speaking to PH, but broke the cleanse one night, and Christmas 2013 became a messy situation of trying to be strong, and yearning so deeply for things to be good and healthy and 'back to normal'.

The thing is, there was never a 'normal', and things were never healthy, ever. But I hungered for it anyway. I spent Christmas Eve at my Aunt's house with my Cousins. And in particular a Cousin/best friend extraordinaire—although she is almost ten years younger than me—who has always been a solid rock in my life. We have always had a very close and special bond.

Christmas morning, December 25, 2013, was just me and my dog, Merlot. We wore matching PJ's and I filled the base of the tree with gifts for him. Truth is, I was so lonely. I felt cursed with aloneness.

We are born alone and we die alone, but at that time I had not come to healthy terms with this concept; I was just plagued with a desperate sense of 'alone'. Just me and my dog, and my broken, shattered heart.

'PH' texted me all weekend, and even invited me to go with him to see his family. I declined, not because I wanted too, but because I knew somewhere in my heart that it was not the healthiest thing for me to do. Nevertheless, I still hoped things would change for us. I longed for fate to rescue us. I pictured all of the dysfunction would vanish and magically alchemize into healthy, open, loving love.

I was delusional. Still.

2014 was right around the corner and many things remained unresolved.

Chapter 28

Tipping Point

2014

"HOPE IS NOT a strategy." That's what my girlfriend, Andrea, used to tell me over and over again. But, how do we plan if we don't have hope? It pissed me off that she would say that because I was so lost in denial and all I felt I had was hope.

But she was right: hope is absolutely not a strategy.

I didn't know it then, so I continued on the path of 'hope'. 'His' texts that Christmas (2013) gave me hope. The Christmas gifts for Merlot from his Mother, and the wrapped box to me from 'him' also gave me of hope. The fact that I was the human he was thinking about while surrounded by family on Christmas day gave me hope.

But he was just playing my heart.

I was right where he wanted me. On New Year's he jetted off on vacation with "the guys" on a snowboarding trip, and only via Facebook did I find out that it was a lie and it was not 'just the guys', I had been played yet again. My hope had been burned by the person who intentionally fed me that promise. And I was a puppet, letting him pull the strings. I was a fool who fell for his tricks over and over.

I told myself I had no right to have feelings toward his trip; we were not together. My anger was irrational. The chemistry of hope—his specialty to experiment on me—had been fueled by gifts, and texts, and messages of love from him; led me to believe something good could come from it all. The reality was, however, that this was a pattern. He could do whatever he wanted with my heart. It evoked incredible shame, for I kept blindly running back for more. 'More' kept knocking me flat on my ass.

Love does not play games. Love does not hurt over and over and over and over. But I only knew that from time to time. I thought the texts, and the gifts under the tree, and the invitation to spend time with his family, was love. And really, you would think I would have known that after all the time I'd been exposed to this kind of game. But my comprehension was weak. I'd been played by a master.

And I'd become an accomplice to my own demise. I was still learning. I was in for the long game. I didn't realize then that the journey to healthy is a never ending voyage. And the longer we travel, the more we learn. If I was going to achieve my calling—healing others—I needed full immersion in darkness; I needed to learn to see the divinity in the darkness so that I could share it.

I remained a mess. Angry, unable to walk away from dysfunction, strangled by the Vine of Anguish. Even 'I' didn't want to be around me. I would have done anything to crawl out of my own skin and walk away from me.

The only place I found joy was at school. The only place I felt truly safe was in therapy sessions.

When I was with PH it felt 'good', but he turned on me so often that I was in a constant state of imbalance; still walking on eggshells.

It was right around this very time too that school was intensifying and we had our first case study due. I met up with one of my close girlfriends, Anise, who took the Nutrition program with me. We went to our favorite vegan restaurant, drank wine, and worked on school work. I told her everything that was going on.

I began to put my story out in the open.

And in a variation of an intervention, after I'd displayed all my shadow aspects in front of my family during the Christmas season, my Aunt took me out on Boxing Day.

She explained that my anger was poison, and that this poison was only hurting 'me'. Though I am certain many other family members wanted to say this to me, and could have, it is likely I would have only listened to her—she had my respect and the timing was perfect.

"I love you so much that I'm going to deliver some of the hardest news your soul can hear. I hope you take it and soar. I hope you heal."

The conversation pushed me further into a sense of self-responsibility. It was time to look in the mirror and deal with me.

Jan 12, 2014

December 2013 was rough. Lots of anxiety, insomnia, and dark thoughts – lots of suicide, self-cutting, drive-off-a-bridge thoughts.

Though I truly never thought I was going to lose it completely, I felt I was close to crossing the fine line, over into insanity.

I moved in with a girl I go to school with (Katie). It's the cutest house. We painted last night. I think this is going to be a major year of healing.

I have not touched booze in two weeks. I think alcohol was becoming a major issue for me and making me really, really depressed.

⋆⇥▱ ▱⇤⋆

There was a woman in my class, Katie. She reminded me—in the best possible way—of a witch. From the first moment I saw her, I knew we'd have a story together.

Katie was everything one could hope to see in a holistic nutrition student. Passionate to a fault. She was pure, and she was opinionated. She carried only reusable bags and mason jars, her hair flowed long in that natural woman kind of way, and she had an array of statement glasses. She was smart; brilliant even.

I didn't know it on that first day of class, but Katie and I would reflect parallel personality traits in one another. She was very particular about how she lived. She had rituals to keep her mind strong, and she was sensitive to the energies around her. She needed sufficient alone time, and things in her life needed to be in a particular order, be it books on the shelf—all sorted by colour and size—or the relationships that she allowed in her heart hemisphere.

Katie and I never fully spoke about her past or all of her opinions, but I knew from being around her that she understood more than she let on. She was a woman that intimately understood the darkness. And, therefore, the darkness did not scare her.

At that time, I was busy wading in and out of my soul swamp, walking the fine line between joy and insanity. I had not come to a place of bliss, nor had I come to the point of understanding the war raging in my head.

Ironically, in January 2014, Katie saw that I'd posted on Facebook that I needed a new place to live. She happened to need a roommate. She came to me one evening at school and asked me if I'd like to live with her. It was a decision I had to consider in that we both had strong personalities. We could mix the way reishi loves chaga or we could repel the way oil resists water; I didn't know. But what I did know was that I had to have a rest from all the drama. I knew, at that point, my inner turmoil had reached full capacity. I recognized the tipping point was not far off.

So I moved in to an old character home. My time living with Katie was short but powerful. One of the most transformational nights of my healing happened in that house with her.

We burned a lot of incense and sage; there came about an intentional cleanliness of energy in the house. It was such a beautiful break from the chaos that I had been used to. I had sworn to a 'Dry January' because alcohol was starting to become a big problem; it affected my coping skills. It was easier to carry out because Katie did not drink at that time.

Through therapy I had been experimenting and learning the effect that creative art has on my psyche. I needed that outlet, it kept me grounded. Until that point my art looked like chicken scratch drawings on blank paper with markers in my journal. This particular night Katie took me to a craft store helped me buy a canvas and paint and we went home that Saturday night and we made reishi cacao elixirs and then painted all night long. It was magic. I didn't know how to paint, but oh! how amazing it felt to listen to music, drink plant medicine, and just let myself flow through brushstrokes on canvas.

I still have that painting.

There was no drama for me that night, and that was totally foreign. Life was beginning to offer me experiences completely opposite to what I was used to. For the first time, perhaps ever, I began to see (almost from an outsider's perspective) how my soul reacted to different stimuli. I was able to begin to come to terms that the drama was killing me. That each time I returned I sunk lower and lower. And I was able to see that, despite being knocked down when I would return, I was addicted to it—the drama. It felt like home.

January 26, 2014

I pray that one day life feels good and on purpose. I pray that one day I do not feel so alone.

I went twenty-four days without alcohol. Feels good. Wine this weekend, but a reasonable amount. Not overdoing it.

⇢▬◉ ◉▬⇠

I hit my tipping point at around the time of my 30th birthday. February 12, 2014. I could not wait to be 30. I'd heard that with each decade we become more self-assured and more grounded. I took that to heart; looked forward to some inner peace. Clung to it. I also knew I'd done a lot of work. And survived. Finally, I felt I could lay the hell-hole of my twenties to rest.

I had stopped talking to 'him' by this point, but my heart was still very much filled with anxiety and darkness. General un-wellness plagued my existence. I decided to find a new place to live as I no longer felt that living with Katie was serving my highest good.

My whole life just felt like survival mode from drama and yet I was also so addicted to it. The chaos was home to me; it felt settling even though the effects of it were very much the opposite.

Some of the things I began to do at that time, in order to maintain my sanity, was to make elixirs, accessing adaptogens—basically herbs known to nurture the nervous system and promote calm. I combined them to craft elixirs to ease my anxiety. I became a regular customer at a store called The Light Cellar, which is a combination "elixir bar"/apothecary.

Attending school was a massive injection of joy in my life, as was engaging with Dr. Joe.

It had come about in therapy that the pain I associated with the 'abuse' was connected to the profound grief I experienced over losing my Dad. Seriously, through all that pain, in all those moments with PH, I might as well have been six years old and reliving my Dad's passing.

I visited the graveyard; a hugely cathartic experience.

I filed the first police report.

Despite engaging in elixirs and good things, I also fought the healthy route. February was a whirlwind of chaos for me. Allergic reactions to food manifested in disturbing ways of depression, insomnia, and anxiety. I tried all kinds of unhealthy ways to escape: cocaine and blackout drinking; one-night-stands undertaken with a distorted sense of self, and the vague hope that I'd be rescued.

I pray that anyone reading this does not take the route I did. I danced with self-hate, learned about self-love, practiced it for a time, fell out of love with myself, and then fought long and hard to find my way back to that sacred state.

Singer Tony Bennett said (referring to Amy Winehouse), "If she had lived, I would have said: slow down; you're too important... Life teaches you, really, how to live it... if you could live long enough..."

There is debate in the coaching and counselling world about whether it is ethical to bring a human into their darkness. When I was studying to be a life coach there was a live debate between the counsellors enrolled in the class and the instructors of the life coaching course about this very topic. The counsellors absolutely disagreed with 'process coaching'—taking a human 'down the tube' and into darkness.

I disagreed with those particular counsellors. My feel is that 'not supporting someone face their darkness' is passive. It does not serve anyone to avoid the meaning of being human.

Facing my shadow was risky—yes, it almost killed me, but in the end dealing with my shadow was my salvation. Surrendering into the darkness and learning deep self-care, compassion, and forgiveness gave my life meaning. Accepting of all that I am—not just the fun, shiny parts—led me to my full-self.

When we ignore our shadow, it gets bigger. We cannot outrun it. It will always be there. We cannot escape our darkness.

**Why have we become so afraid
to look at the pain and discomfort within us?**

Entering the darkness can be dangerous, but equally scary is remaining in a state of inauthenticity—playing small, never facing our fears will zap every ounce of energy; it will take away life in a slow, numbing, and melancholy tide.

We are so accustomed to only seeing the light—or wanting to. We create vision boards, make plans, set goals, all in the interest of seeing the glass half full. We are shamed if we see it half-empty. But what good does that do when we don't even look at the vessel that contains our contents?

We want to fix other people, not ourselves. People want to fix us, not themselves. We want to see life through rose-colored glasses. But when we cannot see at all, then irritability morphs to a permanent negative, tears erupt, a general state of grey moodiness takes over our lives, even depression becomes the norm.

The thing is, life has an entire dark nature to it which we often fail to embrace. We diligently work to ignore it. We numb, we distract, we run, we hide, we do whatever we can to avoid seeing the elephant planted front and center of a room we call 'our living room'—our life.

We are afraid to talk about things like depression, abuse, anxiety, insomnia, self-harm, addictions, abortions, rape, losing our jobs, being broke, anger—for fuck's sake, we are even afraid to talk about orgasms. And heaven forbid we mention bowel movements—pooping— something that should be happening to humans at least once a day. What's sad about this is that not only are we shaming a real part of our humanity, but we are labeling it as ugly and undesirable.

Authenticity and vulnerability are words that are currently trending, as they should be. But how can we show up real and raw if we only accept one part of our humanity?

We only self-love when we are thin, happy, rich, employed, addiction free, in love, having orgasms. That is conditional self-love.

What about unconditionally loving our whole selves? What about embracing radical self-acceptance? What would that be like?

I spent a long time avoiding darkness. I ignored it and suppressed it. I thought it was ugly and undesirable. I didn't know that there was divinity in the darkness. We cannot ignore half of what makes us human, but we can numb it and try to run—I sure did.

I raced away from the darkness toward an imaginary finish line.

I fought the addiction to drama. Weeks turned to months.

In hindsight, I realized I'd been growing ever since my first visit to Marcus, the therapist. And even over more time than that, if I look deeper; it became apparent I had been growing every day, no matter the situation—even dormancy is a phase of growth.

Moment by moment we are offered the opportunity to grow—therefore, we are in a constant state of transformation. And because we are in that ever-growing, always developing, state, then dark or light, it is all an evolution of self.

When I looked into the constellation of myself, I began to understand I could look forward. And once I was able to do that—albeit a slow journey with many setbacks—the darkness comforted me. I found divinity in the darkness.

Only then could I take parts of the Vine of Anguish and press its leaves between pages. Only then could I go back to the earth, get my fingers in the dirt, and uncover Anguish's roots. It was only then that I could recognize the potential of a garden—that parts of that toxic plant could be harvested and used for good; could become medicine. Anguish could be a companion plant to the herbs it once shaded, choked off, and almost destroyed.

Part Two

Night Vision: Trusting The Darkness

In adulthood, the first time my therapist had me close my eyes and visualize my six-year-old-self was heartbreaking.

There I was, with long braided pigtails a little pair of white underwear and no top; dirty from playing in the mud. Innocent, cute, and mischievous to my core.

But this 'little Kori' was different that the one I'd seen in old photos. There was no joy in her. She was sitting on a wooden chair and had her face turned away from me. It tried hard to get a look at her but she would not let me.

There was an undeniable energy of sadness about her. She seemed to be gazing with longing somewhere else, and she certainly didn't want anything to do with me. No six year old girl sits on a chair, in contemplation, with a deep sense of loss, but she did. I couldn't understand.

"What's she doing?" my therapist asked.

"Erm…well… she is just sitting there on a chair, all alone in an empty room. It seems to be a front entry of in a house. She won't look at me", I replied.

"What do you want to do to her?" he asked me.

I murmured, "Hug her, I guess. But I am kind of pissed at her; she won't even look at me. I don't think she likes me."

I stayed in the visualization for a long time; just staring at her while she stared somewhere else. She did not trust me, of that there was no doubt. I should have wanted to save her, or comfort her, or make her innocent six year old self feel better. But instead I was fucking pissed at her; deeply hurt. How could my own self not trust myself? How the fuck was this happening?

And suddenly, in that moment, I knew with full certainty that there was serious work to do.

ONE OF FIVE

Courage

"What would courage have you do?"

Crystal Andrus Morissette

STRANGELY ENOUGH, IN some kind of channeled benevolent act, PH gifted me
my ticket out.

He'd seen a woman on a local breakfast television show. She'd been promot-
ing a retreat. He thought she represented what I had been talking about doing—
healing others. He paid for a ticket and sent it to my email.

The woman was Crystal Andrus Morissette. Her retreat was called Simply
Woman.

Mum and I attended.

Crystal stood in front of a room full of women—something I'd always envisioned myself doing—and the world, as I knew it, shifted under my feet.

That night I lay in a bathtub of tears. Compelled to contact Crystal, I did,
and shared what I was going through. She related to me on levels that comforted
my soul, and said something I will never ever forget.

"What would courage have you do?"

I knew that my life purpose was to be a healer; to engage in a large scale
initiative that would empower women. It was a vision I'd had since I was young.

What would courage have me do?

I knew, the second after the question, that if I wanted to shine the way I
intuitively knew my soul was designed to shine, that 'he' had to be out of the

picture. I completely understood that, in order to find fulfillment and embody my life's purpose, I would have to cut all ties with 'him'.

"What would courage have you do?"

CAM

"If I choose to stay with him I will have to say goodbye to me."

KLH

Though he'd gifted me the workshop, he continued to practice his abusive patterns. The more negative messages he sent, the clearer I became.

Softness

"Nowhere-to-go-and-nothing-to-do. Just be."

Buddhist concept

GROWTH COMES IN soft, slow moments. Too often, we may think we need to spend a year in an ashram in India in order to slow down and learn about ourselves.

Sometimes we might think the perfect teacher must be available with a steady supply of organic foods and customized meditations in order for us to evolve.

But, quite frankly, growth is a lot messier than that.

Growth can be inconvenient. In demanding our attention, growth can interrupt and cause us to experience more chaos—like changing a dance step midway through a routine, we trip and lose the rhythm.

Growth is never simple and straightforward, for every season is the growing season. It's a work in progress: sowing, sprouting, weeding, harvesting, and preparing for the next crop.

I began to question what the chemistry of my brain looked like. I wondered if there was something deeper—organically, biologically—wrong with me.

'Softness' and 'Slow Down' became my two main mantras. They still are. The state of calm does not come naturally to me; I have to consciously work on it every single day.

Softness meant that I would 'slow down' and place my hand on my heart then simply feel it beat.

I would allow myself the space to feel what showed up without the need to label it, judge it, or rush it through my system. Softness meant that I would diligently work on allowing myself to feel human emotions that went far beyond rage, anger, or righteous indignation. It meant that I would surrender to accepting that there are limitless reasons for an emotion to surface. My job was not to understand the 'why' or 'root', but to witness what it was like for me to be human. I began to allow myself to feel all the feels I needed to feel at any given moment. But allowing ourselves to 'feel all our feels', no matter the moment, is underrated. It is needed for healing. It is essential for growth.

This 'move into softness mode' was not a goal-accomplish-check-done list of tasks. There was no rushing it. There was no tangible item, like a trophy, to example achievement. The growth was seemingly invisible. The slow stuff. The painful, nowhere-to-go-nothing-to-do kind of work. It was so frustrating to me. It felt pointless and unproductive.

But I persevered. I added other practices, beginning with using St. John's Wort, (also known as Tipton's weed or Klamath weed): Hypericum perforatum; its medicinal properties are known to aid in mood disorders, (note: some people are advised not to take Hypericum perforatum).

I introduced other rituals. Each day I wore a necklace to work; my Father's. Mum let me use it as a talisman. To me it represented my mantra of 'softness'. Because it was a man's necklace, it hung lower on my chest than it would on a male's, and so, when I casually touched it, I was, in fact, holding my hand on my heart. Through this practice I was able to create space—momentary pauses in chaotic times. I was basically checking in with my heart. When I did, I'd repeat the word, *softness*, in my head.

I cannot say that I knew exactly why I was doing this mantra, other than the simple fact that being a cold, hard, ice-shell of a human was no longer working. I simply had to try something different.

Tapping into the word softness created interesting shifts. In that instant in which I heard myself whisper that powerful word, all the muscles on my face would relax. This reveals how much stress and tension I carried. This is still something I practice and feel.

Softness opened my heart. Softness allowed me to breathe easier. Softness began to reveal my strengths and, at the same time, made me feel utterly vulnerable.

Softness was my key into the world of vulnerability.

Vulnerability to me felt as if my inner-person was inside out and that my heart existed on the outside of my body, rather than caged in my bones and skin.

In the past and up until this point of discovering softness, I was usually on guard, with eyebrows furrowed; I'd engage in a constant state of 'forward thinking', shallow breathing, and loneliness. Once I experienced vulnerability, through my mantra of softness, I felt a connection to myself and to others. My heart was no longer behind walls inside my body; it was outside of me, in a good way. My emotions were easily processed and accessed here and, though it was scary at first, I was surprised to discover this openness was nourishing.

Before this experience, I had always associated 'softness' with femininity: doing the dishes and being a weak, fragile martyr. I thought woman should be forcefully ploughing through life with a fierce 'don't fuck with me 'attitude'. Underneath this cold belief system, I longed for something more. But until I had personally experienced the feeling of vulnerability, I did not understand that the connection I longed for was not connection with another, it was connection with self.

And through this I opened a path to finding myself. I existed in the beating of my heart. My soul spoke in a love language of its own, complete with an angelic tone. My essence existed in the space between all my soul's infinitely loving messages.

It asked me to return home to a divine feminine of nowhere-to-go-and-nothing-to-do so that I could begin to truly inhabit my space—the same space in which the wisdom of the cosmos lies. In mystery. In a celestial darkness.

Goals, drive, action, and direction each have a place of value, of that there is no doubt. But if I was going to succeed at my original goal in therapy—that of 'finding my spark', I was going to have to apply the lessons of slowing down and self-caring.

Nowhere-to-go-and-nothing-to-do. Just be.

And therein lay the birth of my newfound respect and curiosity for the Divine Feminine.

Awareness

As I started to implement 'softness' into my daily practice, I became more susceptible to negative energies. One time, in therapy, after spending a weekend with PH, I sat in the waiting room like I always did until my therapist asked me to come in. All seemed normal. But, when I walked into the room and sat across from the therapist, I felt like that old shell of a human. I was numb and guarded; almost vacant. It was as if my soul had left my body.

About forty-five minutes into the session I suddenly 'appeared' back in my body. It was as if a force had just entered my body, and that force was 'me'. I went from a state of barely comprehending what was being said to me, to being wide-awake, fully conscious, and deeply involved. A light went on. I was fully present.

I will never forget this session, for what happened was so bizarre and something that I had never experienced before. And my therapist's explanation was a powerful one: **He told me that what was probably happening in my 'life' was that, when I chose to spend time with PH, I was probably disassociating.**

I am not a therapist, nor will I ever pretend I am, but what this meant to me was that in order to remain sane around PH, I literally had to leave my body. I would vacate. My soul and higher-self could no longer tolerate the dysfunction, so, for protection, my inner-self simply 'left'—vacated. This was dangerous because a vacant me did not make choices that served my best interest or honour my higher-self.

I began to understand that I was not able to be a soft and open human being in all circumstances. The environment in which I exposed my vulnerable- and delicate-self mattered. Each time I did, I'd have to re-start to repair damage. And I'd restarted so many times that I'd been 'disassociating'.

In time, I learned that I could maintain softness and vulnerability by setting boundaries, understanding them, honouring them, and using a fierce, but loving, strength.

I learned that it fucking matters who we choose to spend our time with. We cannot expect to remain open and soft in a shit storm of other people's moods and drama.

I became selective with whom I allowed my soul to interact with. My sanity and self-love depend on my ability to discern the situations, circumstances and people with whom I commune.

It would take some trial and error, lots of forgiveness and self-compassion, and, of course, time. And, for all that I needed patience.

⇥⊨◉ ◉⊨⇤

July 21, 2014

I write my final for nutrition today. I write it in two hours. It's kind of emotional to think about. It's been a wild two years. I'm looking forward to taking some healing time after this to re-balance and get healthy again. Old habits are creeping in. Stuff like 'checking out' in the way of 'I don't give a fuck' and 'distancing'. But, the good news is it's nothing like it used to be. And, I am aware of it.

I've discovered that I'm gluten intolerant. Gluten makes me crazy. That has been a MAJOR piece of the puzzle. When I don't have gluten I have no insomnia, no scratching, and no depression. Many other symptoms are non-existent or lessened when I am free of gluten.

Femininity

NOT KNOWING A lot about how to embrace the parts of my soul that exhibited femininity, I would spend a lot of my time researching what feminine was. Who was she? Was she a she? What did it look like? How would it act?

Using metaphors and archetypes really helped me comprehend some of the learning tools.

I adored the beauty and fierceness of Hindu goddesses, each elaborately coloured, and magically equipped with many arms and many tools to aid in self-protection.

The goddess I wound up loving is Kali, 'the dark Mother' or 'Mother Goddess'. On first glance she's a bit frightening but, to me, her story is profound. Her black complexion symbolizes an all-embracing and transcendental nature. Her nudity is primeval, fundamental, and transparent—just like nature.

She fights for good by destroying all that is evil. She is the fierce Mother of boundaries. She is a badass goddess.

Kali symbolizes everything I believe to be true about 'woman-energy'. She has been pivotal in helping me develop my inner-warrior.

The symbol of the goddess helped me develop my relationship to the Divine Feminine.

Over time, I not only embraced transformation, I learned how to see in the dark, without night vision apparatus. And I began the most passionate love affair ever—an eternal relationship with myself.

Transformation

"And the day came when the risk to remain tight in a bud was more painful than the risk it took to blossom."

Elizabeth Appell (Lassie Benton)

AFTER FAITHFULLY ATTENDING therapy, I discovered the Vine of Anguish had become bare; no flowers, no buds, no thicket of leaves—the few left were withered. I was able to get down and dig around its base.

Eventually, I drew the root-ball out of the ground—the womb of the plant which still held life inside. I held the sphere close to my heart, and inhaled.

Its masculinity became a sacred part of me.

I wrapped him in burlap.

Then I set about selecting a different spot—with better exposure. I found the perfect place to transplant the Vine; one which would receive proper intervals of light and dark.

I replanted the root-ball, knowing it could be used for goodness, certain the Vine would grow in harmony with all the other plants—those I had already planted in my internal garden, and those I planned to add.

My vision had shifted so much that the plant's structure had undergone a radical change. Through understanding its biology, I'd been able to comprehend its 'healing' properties.

EPIPHANY

In essence I was basically sitting with a closed book of maps to the wondrous and delightful places in me; roads to reality, paths to passion, coastlines of peace. Afraid to open it in case—once the cover was turned to reveal the first map that I'd be committed to a journey. For a great deal of my life I'd shrouded an Atlas of Darkness—hidden it under my jacket, in my suitcase, in my shoulder bag, stored it under my pillow each night—secreted it away. For all intents and purposes I'd buried it.

In therapy, I lost my shit. I completely unraveled over the course of two years. With help, I exhumed the atlas which featured complex versions of the city of me with all its dark alleys, secret gardens, and roads to nowhere, somewhere, anywhere, and everywhere in full cartographic detail.

In therapy, I entered a darkness like none before. I almost died. And through that process I learned that in the darkness exists the secrets to the light. I learned that I am stronger than I ever thought possible. I rekindled my relationship with divinity. I learned to appreciate the shadow side of being human—I learned that if there is light, there is darkness; and if there is darkness, there is light. It was time to explore the other half of what made me human, and I fell head-over-heels in love with me.

I learned that my sole job in my life was to keep my spark alive; I referred to it as my embryo. Through embracing the darkness, I was able to experience the immense capacity to receive love from myself, and from there I discovered my capability to give love.

I freely flipped the pages in the book of maps, carefully unfolding the extensions, gently handling the pop-ups, intently studying the legends, in order embrace it all. And, as I did, signposts appeared, stars became visible, and I used them all to navigate; even started drawing my own maps.

I used garden analogies. I adventured through uncharted territory. I could read the maps in the dark. I coached, I changed lives.

I thrived. I worked hard on my relationship with myself. I surrendered to the darkness and experienced its divinity.

I became lovable, and capable of loving.

Part Three

All The Love: The Divinity In The Darkness

Dear Reader:

**I suppose the reason we're not shown a master plan
is that it would be:
totally overwhelming; b) completely horrifying.**

*No two journeys will be the same. Each heartbeat is individual. But as spiritual philosopher
Ram Dass tells us: 'We are all walking each other home.'*

However you choose to analogize:
We are on the same path, but at different locations.
We are in the same book, just not the same chapter.
We are all in a garden, we happen to grow different plants.
This section is for 'you, you, you' as loved by 'me, me, me'.
May you practice the art of self care and reap a bountiful harvest.

CHAPTER I

Back to the Garden

THE CONCEPT OF the garden can support our journey toward gentle balance and self-care. In the same way we can picture our 'self' as a seed under the ground, we can plant seeds to align ourselves for growth.

If a plant is not cared for appropriately it will die quickly. However, neglected humans die a lot slower. We are more resilient than cilantro, therefore we can get away with neglecting the garden of self for a little longer, or at least it appears that way.

Planting a garden requires:

- Locating a place to cultivate; land with sunshine, shade, and protection.
- Cultivating the land means removing garbage, pulling weeds, turning the soil, and establishing boundaries.
- Choosing the plants. Is yours an herb garden, a wildflower paradise for bees, or a vegetable patch?
- Planting the seeds.
- Nurturing the seed-babies buried deep in Mother-Earth; watering them, monitoring weed growth and soil conditions, and patience. For this is the part where invisible growth happens—we cannot see the seedlings under the ground, we simply have to have faith they are undergoing change.
- Harvesting.
- Site review and preparation for next season.

**"We are stardust, we are golden,
and we've got to get ourselves back to the garden"**

Joni Mitchell, lyrics from Woodstock

The garden is easily related to the patterns of human life.

We must begin by removing garbage, pulling out weeds—the latter an ongoing task. We need to ask ourselves what is harmful to our life-force? What suffocates our roots? What is toxic and stunts our growth?

Weeds in the life-garden are the things that act as energy vampires and leave us feeling depleted. The toxic substances include things we eat, drink, inhale, and think; the overbearing people we associate with, and the abusive relationships in which we are involved. Routines like staying up too late, wasting precious hours watching TV, or skimming social media; essentially the stuff that numbs our minds and distracts us from the truth of our feelings.

We all experience self-destructive habits at one time or another. The task of weeding does not have to focus on an entire forty-acres. All that is needed is to move forward, one row at a time. Removing seemingly small things, over time, create noticeable change.

And, weeds teach us. We have to be careful when we're pulling them up. One form of a poisonous plant might be healthy in another form—eliminating overbearing people is not the same thing as eliminating all socialization. What robs you of your energy might not be what you think. Get to know yourself—it's important you correctly identify 'your' weeds. Becoming the master gardener of your life, your body's botanist, takes a slow and steady approach, much like an apprenticeship.

Once we've recognized certain 'drains' and 'letdowns', then we can add in the appropriate nutrients—the things in our lives that make us feel alive, grounded, and supercharge our purpose.

I emphasize, precious reader, that the only way the 'add in' is possible is via the art of self-awareness. When we have taken the time to self-date and observe, we can then begin to understand our unique needs. Then we can ask: 'What does my soul need?' 'How am I wired to experience contentment and joy?'

It's okay if these answers do not come instantaneously—patience is a large part of the soul of a gardener. Take your time. One seedling at a time. One step at a time. One row at a time.

In the garden we learn patience and stillness, we learn to slow down and have faith. We learn that life happens slowly and there is no rush. We discover that much of our growth is invisible, just like seeds growing under the soil—we cannot see it with our eyes, and yet it is happening, slowly but surely, until one day the shoot pushes through the ground.

The time for the seedling to sprout, to thrive and grow inside the darkness—all that seemingly invisible growth—is equivalent to the process of emotional digestion. Along with swallowing all that pain, and regurgitating it, are the pauses between life-bites. Surrendering, as the seed does in the dark of underground, is growth.

Life is not always about 'set a goal and accomplish it'. The only way to be in positive forward motion is to first truly stop and learn from the dark—just imagine that experience of being that seed underground.

Soul-work is slow and steady, and, more often than not, invisible to the naked eye. When we understand this we're well on our way to a bountiful harvest.

In order to gain perspective we can begin to add things like: breathing deeply – with a 'nowhere to go and nothing to do' attitude—just breathing, journaling, walking, taking in more water, receiving therapy or life coaching. You might find it life-changing to participate in art or volunteer. It can be soul cleansing to clean out a closet, try new, nourishing foods, or savour a good cup of tea. The list is endless: enjoying elixirs, mindful chewing each bite at mealtimes, bathing to relax, going to bed earlier, experiencing more orgasms, praying with purpose—nothing is unachievable and no act of self-care is too small.

The formula for moving forward is always the same whether you are crossing the street or running an ultramarathon: one foot in front of the other and repeat. Every change counts, every step matters.

The process of life-gardening teaches us that finding our weeds—our pains and troubles—then weeding them out or re-categorizing them provides the opportunity to meet our higher-self. Past sickness and drama are a collection of material from which to learn.

WORTHINESS/IN THE COMPANY OF YOUR STELLAR SELF

I am capable of choosing a place in my home that is sacred to me.
It can be two square feet in the corner of a room, a side table off in an unused spot (which you clear of all clutter). Leave it clear, then add what you feel you need. A cushion? A candle? A rock from your own yard? Make this your altar. A shrine to your peace. You can even name this place if you so desire.

I am worthy of ten minutes.
Do a mental search or an internet scan for nearby shops where you could purchase the perfect journal. Look at your calendar and find a space for a date when you will go and purchase one (and where).

I deserve one hour to:
Nap-not-nap. Just lie beside yourself and hold yourself and cuddle. Nowhere to go and nothing to do.

*If you have a favourite beaded necklace or bracelet (no religious symbolism necessary, but rosaries work just fine, too), see if it feels good in your hands, then move your fingers from bead to bead stating a positive word, a prayer, or a name along each one.

Please remember, we are not looking for instant, recognizable change, or gargantuan epiphanies, we are ritualing to be with the self, to get to know who we are, to honour our soul-self. We need still moments to stop and feel ourselves. That's it. Find out who you are in the still moments. Nothing more. Nowhere to go and nothing to do. One foot, and then the next.

Give yourself permission to enjoy half a day to:
Purchase a journal, then spend some time at a coffeehouse with it, just admiring it, soaking in the atmosphere of the place, and you sitting there with your new journal. Take out your pen and record your thoughts and feelings. The purpose of the journal is emotional purging, not perfection. It's not about quality of the writing, the best story, or making it neat and tidy. It is about honouring the buzz that goes on inside your soul. It is about allowing

space for the creative process to accompany and nurture your growth. You do not need to be a 'writer' to keep a journal.

There is always enough time ~ you are the maker of your own time, so:
Sit with your journal and write out responses to these questions:

What do I want more of?
How do I want to feel?
What excites me?
What nourishes me?
What makes me smile?
Who makes me smile?
What adds to my life?
What energizes me?

Take your time. Return to each of these questions frequently, for you are evolving day by day, therefore, so will your answers evolve. Do not mistake the statement: 'you reside within you' with 'you know you'. Each statement is quite different.

Knowing yourself takes time and dedication and practice—just like knowing a lover or a friend would. Respect the changing and evolving version of you by honouring your self-dating ritual. Be comfortable knowing that, day by day, moment by moment, your answers, your needs, your nourishment, and your weeds will morph and change.

**"It's alright
Honey, it's alright
It's alright to be alone."**

Gregory Alan Isakov – lyrics: Honey, It's Alright.

CHAPTER 11

Sacred Self Exploration

IN ORDER TO create boundaries in our lives we need to have a clear image of ourselves, then we can discover what we appreciate and desire. We do not always have a handle on the whole picture so it's vital to spend some of our time in deep self-exploration.

And, we can't possibly ever know the entire story of self because it is ever-evolving. Self-exploration never ends. We are like onions: as we peel back one layer, we find another; infinite stratums. It appears that as long as we remain in human form, we are on the path of discovery.

Self-exploration requires space and silence in order for us to hear the echo of the great void inside.

It requires that we stop where we are at and get still and listen to the beating rhythm of a dedicated heart. Slowing down can feel counter intuitive, unproductive, even a waste of time, but by not engaging in slow evaluation we can truly become disconnected.

There's a lot of value placed on forward movement. Society places little worth on sinking into the spaces in which we currently reside. Too busy with goals and visions of the future, we've forgotten the meaning of the moment. We've abandoned the pleasure of tasting life and breathing in adventure—we've let go of the feeling of the subtle vibrations of being human. We have forgotten the magic in the mundane.

Few of us think about how we do not exist in tomorrow. We let 'this moment' speed by to plan for advance moments. But it is only in the here and now that we can appreciate being alive. Tending the heart is actually simple, what complicates the process is our obsession on the tomorrows and the yesterdays. This looking ahead and looking back disregards the 'right here and NOW'.

What needs to be cared for right now? Stay in the now. Stay with the beats of the heart—the inhales and exhales—and you will find the answers one moment, one breath, one step at a time. Remember: nowhere to go and nothing to do.

In a world that values speed, business, productivity, rapid advancement, our obsession with accomplishments and forward drive are a strong addiction to avoidance. We are experts at evasion because in those silent spaces, where we let go and seemingly do nothing, the vastness of the capabilities of the human heart becomes apparent. It's not an easy task to feel the feels. And that's what we do in those silent spaces. Feeling the feels is a task for a warrior, a warrior just like you, the one reading these very words.

It is in the silent moments of self-exploration that all the 'feels' bubble to the surface; all the joys and the wounds, excitement and sorrows, all pool into conscious awareness.

But, without slowing down, without connecting to the heart, we cannot know self-love, understand self-care, or offer our human selves the level of self-compassion required to uncover our innate ability for unconditional self-love and forgiveness.

There will be a time and a place that life demands you to finally slow down. One can only live off of the spoils of excitement, accomplishments, and drama for a period of time, Without the pause, without the slow down, and completely lacking cultivation of magic in the mundane, the soul will remain only partly known. There will continue to be a missing piece on the puzzle of your self-care. The soul will, at some point, demand we honour the productive space of slowing down.

→▬● ◉▬←

For me, therapy was essentially the opening of a garden gate.

At each session, my therapist would ask me to anchor my feet firmly on the floor, place my hand over my heart, close my eyes, and simply breathe.

The transformation from scattered, self-deprecating thoughts, chaos, and drama, to the profound awareness of the heart beating under my hand took my breath away. Every. Single. Time.

When I felt my heart under my hand, I'd cry. I'd sob for the joy I felt and simultaneously for the losses I'd endured. I'd weep over the miracle of the body and the related sorrow for having ignored my heart for so long. I'd marvel at the sheer miracle of our human body—and express pure gratitude for the intricate, intelligent system.

Whenever I consider the science and wonder of it all, I cannot help journey to the cosmos. I remain in awe of whatever great mystery created this entire structure of complicated, intricate magic.

And each week, when my hand was over my heart, I'd find great peace in knowing that no matter how badly I'd screwed up my week, no matter how off-course I'd wandered, regardless of how many self-hateful thoughts I'd battled, my heart—my dependable, loyal, precious heart—kept beating.

No matter how hard it was for me to leave the abusive partner in my life, no matter how many tears I shed, or glasses of wine I drank, there was a constant rhythm in my chest.

It didn't matter if I was "good girl" who diligently worked toward and envisioned a 'finish line', and it didn't matter if I said all the right things, and pleased all the humans in my life. None of it was relevant, because my heart proved itself by continuing to beat.

My heart's commitment to me was unconditional. It held space for me when I couldn't give my attention to any life-enhancing practices. It directed me, from its dependable place of peace to explore options of further serenity. It was patient.

-→▣ ▣←-

My organs, and your organs, need tender love in order to function optimally. This requires appropriate exercise, positive thought patterns, stress management, sleep, hygiene, emotional competency, nourishment in the form of high-quality food, and other essentials tailored to each individual.

When we hold our hand to our heart and close our eyes we can ask: "What does my heart need now?"

It might direct you to rest. It might ask another to pray. Sometimes it might suggest a walk, and other times compel a person to write. There will be times when that 'daily check-in' simply provides the opportunity to shed tears.

It's okay if the 'check-in' creates a blank 'I don't know how I feel'. What matters is the act of checking in, the act of saying "I am worthy." The practice of stating, "I care to know myself". That's what matters most. Not some epiphany, or an expected outcome.

It's so cliché, but it truly is the journey, not the destination, that is the most important. The intention to enter into self-care provides the catalyst for awareness. The resulting participation yields profound peace.

And no matter what that dependable, phenomenal organ answers, take care not to judge its answer; simply learn to allow what is delivered to move through you. If rage and anger shows up, honour it. All of the heart's messages are stepping stones to a greater picture of peace. They may seem, in the moment, like nothing, but they are the clues to our ability to self-connect and thus to connect with others, our life purpose, and the world.

If I did not listen to my body and I ignored the spirit, then it would speak louder in the form of emotional outbursts, 'bad luck', and physical symptoms. The desires of the mind, body, and spirit will be heard one way or another—that is the way it functions. It helps guide us to our soul-work.

The body truly acts as an emotional compass. It will faithfully—all of the time—signal being off course via symptoms, moods, and cravings; clear signs that something inside needs tending. The answer can usually be found by checking in with the heart. The solution is always in embracing the pause.

Conveniently and ideally, it is from an internal garden of peace that we learn there is **nowhere to go and nothing to do**. Sometimes moonless nights in, among, and under the seeds and plants of our life is exactly the nourishment we need.

For we are stardust, and we are golden, and it's so important we each find our way back to our garden.

I land on heart.

In the company of your stellar self you are worthy of fifteen minutes:
Get comfortable, hand over heart, and ask 'what does my heart need now' then wait, just sit and wait… and wait… It may take some time for you to hear; that is perfectly normal—the thing is: at least you are willing to listen, and your heart will know that and begin to whisper to you.

Cultivate patience. This is a practice, and just like you would not take on a new sport and expect immediate perfection, so too will this practice remain just that… a practice.

Slow and Steady. One foot and then the next. Remember: this is not a race. Nowhere to go and nothing to do.

You are absolutely worthy of one hour:
Craft an elixir with ingredients you have on hand. If you have a lemon and water, so be it, an elixir of lemon and water. If you have some herbs, infuse them, blend others—become a little or a lot witchy. Sip and enjoy. Look into books or online information about plant medicine you would like to grow or purchase. Seek local suppliers who can support your purchases, and who are ethical and knowledge-able, such as the Light Cellar in Calgary. Choose only one item, two at the most. This is not meant to be overwhelming or taxing.

And what, you may ask, is an elixir? My own definition is this: a healing and magical plant-based potion crafted to nurture the body, mind, and soul.

Your phenomenal self can deliver a gift of an entire day, just for you:
Can you imagine? One entire day Just. For. You?

Cultivate this as a habit. You need it. You deserve it.

Plan the whole day for you. Take yourself out on a date. Visit inspiring places—even specialty stores—go to the museum or library, enter a church, a park, a forest, an historic building, or take in the ambiance at a public venue showcasing art. Collect pebbles—the day doesn't have to cost any-thing. You can even take a thermos of elixir you make for yourself. Bring along your journal. Wear your favourite outfit—just like you would on a date with a lover. This is a rendezvous with your greatest romance and soul-mate: yourself.

Treat yourself to a healthy, warm beverage or an icy smoothie. Indulge in flavours that pleasure you. Go slowly, savouring each mouthful. Seriously, pick the food you love... rally around that food; love and savor it, enjoy it, thank Mother Earth for it and, for heaven's sake, stop beating yourself up bite by bite. Let that shit go and give yourself permission to receive pleasure in the form of food flavors, whichever tickle your fancy.

Enjoy your own company. Flaunt that enjoyment. Smile at strangers, by all means; wave at train drivers. However, resist distraction; retain boundaries to only entertain and cherish yourself. This is your opportunity—and be sure to know it is not a chance, it's an opportunity of immense proportions and incredible consequences—to be selfish... divinely self-centered. Selfish with the intention of self-knowing, self-dating, and self-compassion, because, guess what? when you hone in on your love for you, you end up with more love to give to the world. The world needs you to get divinely selfish. The world needs you to shine. And when you shine you are ready for your life's purpose. That only happens when your love tank is full. And it's a self-serve pump, Sister. Your love tank becomes full by the love you give to self.

You are creative enough to design a mini-series of worthshops for yourself:
Begin a routine time-slot—to be decided by you, three weeks in a row. Behave as if you are going to a course you've signed up for. It can be outside your home in your favourite coffeehouse, or it can be inside your home in your sacred corner.

Choose three topics you want to explore. Here are three suggestions:

1. Who were you as a child, where is she now? What happened to her?
2. What stops you from doing things—who is your inner saboteur and what does he/she/it look like?
3. Who, inside yourself, champions you—what does your inner warrior look like?

Dive into each of these questions and make each a project: a creative endeavor.

Get to know your inner child. What does she look like? What does she love doing?

When your inner-child is around, how do you feel?

Who is the saboteur? If the saboteur was a fairy tale character, who would they be?

When your saboteur is around, how do you feel?

What do each whisper in your ear?

How about your inner-warrior? Who is she? What does she look like? What does she want for you? Paint Her! Draw Her! Collage Her! Get creative—don't miss the details.

These are the parts of you that can guide you in the light and through the darkness.

CHAPTER III

Feminine Energy

WHEN I BEGAN to go deep into my soul to connect with the concept of feminine energy it was as foreign to me as if I'd boarded a flight to outer space. It may well feel that way for you too.

One of the first activities I decided on was to create a 'goddess bath'. I filled my tub with all things that smelled good—essential oils, Epsom salts, organic bubble-bath products. Once I'd created the cauldron, of sorts, I'd immerse myself and then stare at the ceiling—total quiet time.

The thing is; once I was in that tub, I didn't know what else to do other than stare at the ceiling. The whole 'self-care' and 'self-knowing' thing was overwhelming, intimidating, and fucking scary. My brain told me it was a stupid waste of time. But I did it anyway.

I had to do it anyway—I knew that by always 'doing it my own way' I had been swallowed by darkness. Those days that I had resisted slowing down and stepping out of the drama were beyond hazardous to my health. And so I was gifted exhaustion. And I unwrapped it—tentatively—and the present revealed itself.

Now I know—through rituals—how to preempt that exhaustive, depressed state. It's my wish that you learn how to do that too.

It was in my quiet time that I learned the value of creating an exterior space that matched the interior places I wanted to go. In other words, as I worked on inner calm I began creating a clean living space. I included artwork and that reflected the desires of my heart. Through this, my home-space became a living altar; a sacred place for me to surrender.

In the early days of cultivating all-things-self, I fumbled around, dancing with two left feet. I truly 'faked it until I made it'. I didn't know what worked or what my sacred altar needed to look like, so I started, metaphorically, throwing spaghetti at the wall to see what stuck.

Try that, the more you toss at the wall the sooner something will stick; and please don't be fooled into thinking that the pieces that do not stick are a 'waste of time'. Hardly! All the pieces will help shape your altar. They will each represent your journey in honouring your 'self'. Your self-care rituals will evolve into exactly what you need. Be patient. Be slow.

And, in the quiet time, I engaged with my love for plant medicine and crafting potions and elixirs. I spent countless hours at the Light Cellar—a Calgary business which offers a massive range of superfoods. Its café/apothecary environment, with a warm, caring, and knowledgeable staff, further inspired me.

Most of the time I went to there alone—it became a hallowed space for me to let down my walls. I would walk up and down the aisles of magical plant medicines and simply celebrate the joy of being close to the natural qualities and properties for which I had so much respect. I interacted with those who worked there, and indulged in picking their glorious brains.

The shop became a sanctuary for me. I went there so many times feeling anxious and overwhelmed, but in minutes that that disquiet disappeared. It may not have made sense to others—hell, it barely made sense to me, back then—but I felt as if I had 'come home'.

Row by row, shelf by shelf, I took inventory of the store and, at the same time, I suspect I was truly inventorying my 'self'. The process was medicine for my soul. At the time, all I knew was something about being there felt right, and so, that is where I continued to return. I didn't question it. I trusted my soul and, through that, I honoured the sacred, inner-request.

Crafting potions and elixirs became an expression of love and authenticity. I shared it with others, but I also practiced the crafting as a sacred ritual, on my own.

Through the healing space I created, I'd find myself drawn to my Dad's grave. I kept a yoga mat in my car specifically for visits to the site. It too became a sanctuary of sorts, where I could cry, laugh, and tell my father about therapy, my life, and my day. All questions went unanswered, but it felt good to be there.

There was one day, on the way to the gravesite, when I stopped at the Light Cellar for an elixir—to-go. I told one of my favorite people who worked there that I was heading out to forage for magical material to make a magic wand; a homework assignment I created in therapy. He gifted me a piece of reishi to add to my wand.

I accepted it with gratitude and added it to my wand-making supplies and headed to my Dad's grave. Sitting there in front of his grave on a yoga matt with a mason jar filled with plant medicine in the form of a tasty elixir, and a bag full of magic wand-making supplies, I laughed at how crazy I must have looked; but I was at home in that moment. Nothing else mattered.

I felt more like me than ever before.

I practiced worthiness through affirmations. Many were those taught by advocate, motivational speaker, and author, Louise Hay.

"Kori, I love you and accept you exactly as you are."

At first I felt like a fraud saying it. I never felt good enough or smart enough. I never thought I would ever find light in my life again. I simply felt like I never measured up.

But, the more I engaged in things that were good for me, the better I started to feel. It was the simple little tasks that slowly but surely started to reignite my soul.

Reading all the 'self-help', spiritual, psychological, heal yourself books I could get my hands on; going to therapy; sitting in the darkness in tears; talking to my inner child; drawing; crafting elixirs; going for runs; teaching bootcamp, seeing my naturopathic doctor; saying morning prayers of gratitude, and also saying a prayer for myself and the world—each of these actions were manageable and valuable; they led me deeper into self-love.

It's important, even urgent, for me to emphasize that, at the time, all of this 'stuff' was so foreign; it all seemed so purposeless. But my life was not working under my terms; I needed something new. I followed the practice because I needed to be teachable and willing. I carried out all the small things—tiny acts—that I could not fathom would lead me anywhere.

But they did lead me somewhere. And not just anywhere. They led me home to my heart and soul.

Slowly, but ever so surely, I started to kind-of-sort-of like the human that I was. I became proud of my growth and ability to look in the mirror and face what needed to be changed. I felt pleased to feel human emotions, something I had not known I was capable of. I was fulfilled that no matter how much I had drank, or how badly I had fucked up, or how many frigging times I had returned to him (PH), I had still showed up to therapy, and never abandoned my work. I took my work very seriously, and I was really proud of that.

It was in the moments of exploring how far I had come that I started to develop a feeling of self-achievement which, in turn, sparked self-love. My garden began showing the promise of a loving harvest.

And so it was not surprising that my understanding of femininity and the requirement for balance between masculine and feminine was delivered through Mother Earth.

Plants symbolically taught me the importance of equilibrium; masculine and feminine.

To me the roots represent the masculine; they are connected, grounded, driven and strong. They protect and anchor the plant. They are its life force. They speak to me of masculine strengths.

Then there are the leaves and the flowers—feminine strengths; the parts of the plant that are exposed and vulnerable. Soft and delicate, they are also surprisingly fierce and strong. A blade of grass can grow through concrete. Vicious storms can come and go, yet delicate leaves and willowy stems remain intact. The sheer strength blows my mind.

In that perfect balance, the roots are part of the plant's life force as is the greenery which is responsible for photosynthesis.

The masculine needs the feminine and the feminine requires the masculine.

Feminine energy is not passive and martyr-like. A woman is not a doormat or a meek, weak version of human. She is bold and strong and open and nurturing. She invites the divine masculine to dance. She is self-assured. She is sexual and passionate. She knows how to say NO and when to say yes. She respects rest, and can balance it with fertility and creation. She has an intimate relationship with pleasure, a phenomenal ability to receive it, and a tremendous capacity to heal because of it.

My representation of the feminine was an embodiment of a Hindu goddess; glorious, radiant and welcoming, and well-equipped, with her many arms and weapons, to defend her personal boundaries.

I slowly started to play with my comprehension of what it meant for me to be a woman. I began to value and admire the divine feminine, and I do not just mean solely in women. I began respecting the men—all the humans—who had found the balance of masculine and feminine in their hearts.

Discovering the power of femininity has changed the course of my life and given me permission to fall into a profound state of love with myself. It is a work-in-progress.

It took a combination of surrendering into where I was at, and acknowledging and witnessing my level of self-loathing, while simultaneously peeling myself out of my goddess bath, to face the world and do something that was good for my soul.

What is the strength of femininity?

What do you believe to be the qualities of femininity?

Who, in your life, exudes these qualities?

What/who are your top 'feminine role models'? (Think about people you know, include those with celebrity status, too. Choose characters in fiction or in film. What of the women in history?)

→⟫◎ ◎⟪←

I serve myself well by making time to enjoy my passions. In under five minutes:
Close your eyes and whisper the word 'softness'. Take note of how you feel and what images appear. Breathe naturally, let your body fall into softness. If resistance shows up to this word, that's okay too, just notice it. Your job as a self-gardener, in this part of the process, is to simply observe. Become aware of who you are moment to moment.

You are deserving of one hour of exquisite self-love:

Run yourself a bath, add something pure to it. It may be a bundle of rosemary tied under the tap, or it might be a selection of natural products you have been inspired to combine. Relax into the water and use the ceiling as your blank canvas. Be gentle with yourself as you paint pictures of your desires on the 'screen' above you. Let yourself dream. Relax. Let yourself feel.

Seriously, you can't fuck this up, there is no wrong way to goddess bath.

Long weekends are for long-lasting love:

Book a trip to the mountains or a place you enjoy. Take your journal.

OR

Create an uninterrupted weekend at home and fill it with a slow-paced retreat schedule with lots of time for nothing to do and nowhere to go. Have some self-help movies on hand. Louise Hay's, *You Can Heal Your Life* is an excellent example. Plan your food. Pamper yourself for the entire weekend. If you feel stuck in planning such a weekend ask yourself this: "If I were to pick a retreat to attend, what would I be looking for?' (food, activities, down time, the forest, weather, alone time, sisterhood time, creativity…) then plan your weekend based on a "dream retreat". Write it out. Follow through with the preparations, stick to your schedule. This is your retreat.

OR

Modify it, cost-wise, in this way:

If you know a friend is heading out of town, arrange to stay at his or her home (especially if your house is too full).

CHAPTER IV

All The Love: The Larger View

BEFORE WE CAN look at the bigger picture, we must take care of the root-system of our home lives. For many of us, there comes a point in our lives where we stop doing the simple things we used to do—from wearing bright colours to doing our hair, or taking the time to sing and dance.

When this happens, we go into a courage deficit. We begin to miss the brave, outgoing humans we used to be, or were meant to be. In some cases, when we abandon that part of our 'self', the 'missing' manifests in feeling unworthy. Simply wearing a nice outfit just because we feel like it becomes a thing of the past; each time we skip over something seemingly small, and substitute 'settling' for 'embracing' we lose a little bit of ourselves. Let me remind you, Sister, there is no step too small, no seed too insignificant. All those 'mini-embracements' add up. They all matter.

Losing a little bit of ourselves 'here' and 'there', by settling instead of embracing, also creates a domino effect—homes become disorganized as does home-life, which affects the way individuals and families share time, organize healthy meals, and enjoy time together.

Yet, it's hugely ironic: we who lose ourselves by abandoning the simple things are the very people who expect to accomplish mammoth tasks like leaving a dysfunctional relationship, quitting a job, starting a business, or moving to another city.

When we can't even dress to feel fantastic for ourselves, when we cannot keep an organized home, how will we be able to deal with much larger issues?

That's right, everything counts. When we devalue our self-worth to an extreme that we cannot even sew a missing button on a shirt, we cannot expect to start a new business; both require a measure of self-worth in order to begin.

In order to reclaim the self-worth we have lost, boost what little is remaining, or even establish healthy self-worth that may never have been present, we have to start in the rooting system. The seeds of self-worth. The seemingly small, but significant tasks. We must be vigilant on the small steps in order to propel us to the heights to wish we wish to soar. Simply said, we must learn to walk before we can run. We have to take care of the day-to-day tasks with intention, love, and ritualistic effort. We have to fill the day-to-day of our lives with pleasure, and beautify it, for it is in the momentary honouring of ourselves that we can embody the expansion of our truest purpose.

Start on the small stuff.

Simple things include starting at home—the location in which you live.

Little by little, organize your home.

- Make your bedroom a sanctuary for deep rest and amazing solo or partner sex—yes, you are worthy of the kind of ambiance that supports solo sex; not everyone has a partner. Ensure your bedroom is set up for that which supports peaceful sleep and satisfies your need for sexual intimacy. Only items which complement these modes of relaxation and expression should be there.
- Oh, and clean out your closet. Make it minimal. Every single item should bring you joy. Every piece should represent your values. Each one an expression of your joy; a visual demonstration of your favourite colours and fabrics. If an item has a negative memory attached to it, or doesn't make you feel radiant, donate it or consign it. And, for those of you with groups of clothing in every size your body inhabits—this physical and mental clutter has to go.
- Choose clothes that fit, and that make you shine.
- Fill your bathroom with affirmations of self-love in the form of products that nourish you; items which reflect and respect Mother Earth.

Get rid of old products that simply take up shelf-room. Seriously, stop hoarding 'stuff'. This 'stuff' clutters your mind and stifles your creative potential.

- Surround yourself with art that inspires you, smells that ground you, textures you enjoy, music that evokes emotion—whether that is total relaxation or the get up and dance the night away kind.
- Get serious with your self-care and sacred surroundings by getting rid of all the junk you intuitively know you do not need.

All these steps allow us to become informed participants in our own lives.

And yes, this is cliché, but live each day like it is your last.

Life is big. Self-work can be daunting—and let's be real: there are simply parts that are out of your control. Period. Self-Care starts by focusing on that which you do have control. Make it simple. These tiny steps matter. Feel overwhelmed and don't know where to start? Pick a room in the house. Identify its purpose, and then remove every-last-thing that does not bring you joy. For real. Do it with the kind of energy you would if you were moving out. Box it all up. Then add back into the 'new' space, because this *is* a move—an energy shift.

Never stop asking yourself: What are the things I love? Who is the inner person I miss—whom I long for? What did 'that person' used to enjoy doing? Am I honouring myself by living a full life and appreciating myself? Do not take this work of self-dating with a single grain of complacency. You are evolving every moment of every day; it's important to continue to check in with self. It's essential you make it your job to know your 'self' better than any 'one' or any 'thing'.

A helpful strategy to use is to become the best 'quiz-master of self ever'. The nosiest busy-body and peeping Tom in your own life. Be your own best friend and ask yourself: Do I care for who I am? When was the last time I let myself dream? Do I dance? Is my life where I imagined it would be when I was a small person—better or worse? What needs to change? What do I long for?

Keep questioning. Am I having fun? Am I laughing a lot? Am I crying enough? Am I getting a decent amount of hugs each day? Am I goofy? Do I hug trees?

Am I nourishing my body with delicious and whole foods? Am I enjoying all foods without guilt or self-deprecating thoughts.

Changing the things we think are small things—which are never small things—become the most benevolent acts we can ever bestow upon ourselves. These 'tiny' things become our Rituals of Self Care.

As 'things' are disposed of, consider letting go of 'labels'.

We wear a lot of masks, as human beings. Shedding the masks and finding 'who' wears them has been an important part of my journey, and can be equally vital to your own journey.

I am not my gender, my age, or my job title. Nor am I the people with which I surround myself. I am not just a daughter, sister, coach, or friend. I am not the food I eat or diet I follow. I am not the books I read or the thoughts I think. I am not my looks, nor am I the number of kilometres I can run. I am not my failures or my accomplishments. I am not my mood swings or my health issues. I am not a lot of individual things or the sum of them.

I am the observer underneath all the things I am not.
And in being the observer,
and not being a part or the sum of ten-thousand things to judge
myself about, I simply exist in the form of two words:
I AM.

For too long my own identity was wrapped up in the people I spent time with, what I deemed to be a successful career, or what kind of education I had. It may well be the same for you.

My identity was wrapped up in the names I had been called. My idea of self was wrapped up in hustling for too many people's opinions of me. I had no idea who I was because I was busy pleasing people and making sure I had approval.

If the crowd liked it, I did it. I couldn't say no. I would wrap myself in each relationship as if it was a heavy, protective coat—the kind worn on the coldest winter nights with the most extreme wind-chill factor. I was too afraid to take off the coat for I had no idea what I would find—who chose to hide—under the opinions of others.

Finding myself saved me.

Getting to know how I operate in my own psyche and soul has been fundamental to my well-being. Learning to say 'no' and then sitting with the discomfort without acting on it has been life-saving.

Understanding my values and how I uphold them through my choices and actions has been the only way I have gained clarity on my identity.

Quiet moments in self-exploration and dates with my true-self to get to know my spirit who lives in this miraculous, thriving package of skin and bones has enabled me to comprehend where I end and where others begin.

Knowing who I am means I can make choices based on my own well-being. I can feel when situations and people cause me to feel off-kilter, and I am capable of saying 'no'. I have clearer boundaries which makes me an excellent participant and show-er-upper. I have intentions not expectations. All this is because I started with the small things that are not small things. The rooting. Putting my 'house' in order.

You are deserving of:

Five minutes to choose a couple of questions from the above section and then set aside—schedule—time for exploration.

List the 5 questions that you plan to explore:

1

2

3

4

5

Describe your self-date in which you will explore these questions:

(where will you go? What elixir will you craft? What will you wear? What time of the day will you reflect? What music will you play? What oil will you diffuse? ...

Delight in a field trip to:

Take an hour to look at the image of the roots of a tree or small plant (real or photographic). Study the 'branches' that go off in directions, the science and wonder of it. Take that image into yourself and begin to picture how you would like to transplant and re-root yourself. Stand and imagine roots expanding from your feet and going deep into the ground. Draw energy from Mother Earth. Journal what it feels like when you connect with that energy. Give yourself permission to belong to 'her'. If you struggle, let it simply be, ask yourself what you are avoiding and how best to get past barriers—then let it go and let the answers flow to you when they are ready.

What soul do you need?

What nutrients would help you grow?

Where will you transplant your roots?

What does mother Earth energy feel like?

What is the power of Mother Earth?

What comes up with you think about the notion of 'self-permission'?

What shows up as you read these questions?

Be real & honest. Your answers are your current truth.

You are worthy of a lifetime of restorative sleep, so set aside an afternoon of Grace, and:

Evaluate the place you sleep…your bedroom. Is it for rest and intimacy, or does everything else take place there (studying, watching television, computer)? Recline on the bed and envision what would have to happen to the bedroom for your sacred needs of sleep and intimacy. Then, make the plan and do it, or schedule a time to do it. It's amazing how much difference an afternoon can make.

Short on space? Then find a way to make a screen so that the space around the bed is serene. Then organize the rest of the room by eliminating things you don't need, reassigning 'stuff' to other parts of the house, or finding the most organized and attractive way to keep what you do want so that its storage supports your serenity.

Creative ideas and questions:

- Think of your favourite hotel room, what made it amazing? Get creative and decide how you can incorporate the qualities of that room in your home.
- Create Pinterest board or a collage of bedroom inspiration.
- What does 'rest' mean to you? What do you think of what you think of rest? (colours, smells, textures, flavors...)
- Are your sheets clean? New? Comforting?
- What about your PJ's? Do you wear any? If not, what kind of self-loving lotion do you use at night? If you do wear PJ's are they nice? Do you enjoy getting ready for bed?
- Intimacy – what do you do/use for self-intimacy? Do you have a yoni egg or sex toys? Is your bedroom set up for love – self-love and partner love?
- What is the theme and ambiance of your room now? What would you like it to be? What needs to be weeded out, and what needs to be added to make this happen?

CHAPTER V

About Rituals

A RITUAL IS a set of actions conducted routinely in the same manner. We all have many that we don't recognize as such.

Although rituals, in general, are perceived as acts of self-discipline, it is important to recognize that human beings thrive on routine.

Self-loving rituals are essentially sets of boundaries that we establish to fully live our own lives.

In this work of self-love and healing, 'ritual' always refers to the intentional practices dedicated to self-care.

Anchored in love, a ritual is a practice created to drive us home to our own hearts; a ritual is like an elixir for our lives.

The thing that I find fascinating is that it is not just the ritual that is important, it is the time allocated to practice, and the dedication to showing up. It is the space between the beginning and the end of the ritual that acts as a statement to the self-saying:

"I am worthy of the time it takes to practice my ritual"

"I am worthy of showing up for myself"

Through loving intention, within the time and space set aside for the ritual, we are lead to a deeper understanding of who we and what we need at the soul level.

Throughout my journey, I discovered numerous rituals. I want to share them with you to spark your own creative capacity to dive into your heart centre so your higher-self will reveal to you unique approaches to your individual and sacred self-love routines.

'Daily Practice'. This phrase is completely credited to my therapist as is much of the success of my journey.

I love using the word ritual; it seems magical to me. It's witchy and whimsical and I believe that when we find ways of doing our lives with added magic and love, our practice become easier. This is why I choose to use fine china for my meals, and why I consciously plate my food with artistic care—it becomes more enjoyable, even glorious, to eat that way.

When you participate in your own life with 'intention' you can begin to establish rituals that support your growth. You can choose wonderful people to spend time with. You can purposely choose the best ingredients, the fanciest wine glass, activities that light your soul on fire.

The daily-practice is unique to each human, it is a personalized ritual that is performed in honour of self-care and connection. Self-care rituals are as important as breathing, for they are life sustaining.

When I first began daily practice of rituals of self-care I made a big mistake. I thought I needed to over-achieve, and was armed with a massive list of unattainable to-do's. Because, well, if we are going to make one change we might as well make *all* the changes, right? Wrong. Dead wrong. Well, I got nowhere quickly. Well, that's not fully true; I arrived at 'overwhelm' almost immediately, and had a strong desire to quit.

Rituals do not need to be overwhelming. In order to incorporate rituals into daily practice they must be simple and fit into the schedule of your unique life.

Each ritual has to be concise so that it can be practiced daily. These rituals are small acts, smaller than you think they should be. Teeny. Tiny. Miniscule. Minute. Molecular. At the cellular level—that small! The whole, 'if a butterfly wing changes the breeze on the other side of the world' ripple effect kind of thing.

It is important that we treat our relationship with our own self just like we would with a friend or a lover. We go on dates with our friends or lovers, we bond with them, we carve out special time to connect, to talk and to create memories. Our relationship with the self is no different. It requires space, dedicated time and a willingness to look deeply inward to discover that which makes our hearts light up. This is all done through things like our daily-heart-check-in, self-exploration through things like journaling and tending to our self-garden and of course our daily-practice.

In the darkest nights of my soul, my daily practice was simple. At that time in my life I couldn't handle a whole lot more than a daily check-in with myself. This may be how you are feeling. And that is okay. Even just checking in with yourself can be vastly emotional and exhausting. But in recognizing that, there can unfold a daily practice of rest. You may do this by choosing a comfortable spot or creating a 'Goddess bath'.

Eventually, you will be able to add more rituals.

Perhaps you'll use a cup, saucer and teapot instead of a chipped mug.

Perhaps you'll sit in much loved spot in your home when you drink your tea or coffee.

The words I use to describe all of my self-care practices—my rituals—is the Golden Fork Mentality. Simply stated, everything you do for yourself should be like tasting life from a golden fork. Why do we insist on holding back on the 'nice candles' or the 'fancy dishes' for that *one special* opportunity? Every day is special. The gift of each day is the catalyst for sacred rituals; this is key to the journey of self-love.

Rituals have to be filled with self-love because:

1) Life is too short not to be glorious and wondrous;
2) In making everything a Golden Fork experience, one begins to feel deserving of goodness, and then the sense of worthiness grows.

The Golden Fork Mentality allows a little light into the 'ordinary'. In Golden Fork moments we can treat ourselves as if we are royalty. We don't have to sit in a bathtub of plain water to rest, we can invest in organic oils and Epsom salts and then truly luxuriate. Even if you don't feel like a Goddess, please, treat yourself as you are one. If you treat yourself like one, you will feel like one.

When we practice self-care, we master self-love.

In my case:

• I repeated affirmations in the mirror. I rehearsed treating myself kindly, I role-played being my own best friend, I imagined the garden and tended to my heart as a precious plant which required nurturing and feeding.

- I stretched my comfort zone and engaged some trust, allowing emotions to show up without judging them as uncomfortable and weird (because that is how they felt when they showed up).

- I practiced self-forgiveness, and believe me, I had ample opportunities to practice this one. I worked on self-compassion. I wasn't necessarily looking for "self-love" at that time, I was simply trying not to die.

- And at times I felt like a fraud. I did not feel like a goddess, I did not always believe the affirmations I said, and many times I felt unworthy of this practice. But it's just that—a practice—and, with time, parts of me slowly, but surely, began to embrace these rituals, stepping into the calling of self-care. I truly began to love the skin I was in. I began to fall in love with the eyes—and all they mirrored—that looked back at me each morning as I rehearsed and practiced my affirmations.

Interestingly, I noticed a disturbing pattern: dedication Monday to Thursday, then falling deep and hard from Friday to Sunday.

Though I know a lot of people engage in, for example, healthy eating on weekdays and binging on the weekends—two steps forward and one step back—mine was a more pronounced ten steps back. The troubling aspect of this, for me, was that the more I was dedicated to the two steps forward, and the more my practice nourished my self love, the more heart breaking and damaging those 'ten steps back' became. As I grew emotionally and spiritually, those 'ten steps back' actions that used to be 'okay' ceased to remain natural and, in fact, jolted my soul. A larger part of me demanded that I straighten up and do my damned work.

And, with that awareness I was able to engage in 'every moment' not just a set five days on and two days off.

A typical day for me now, in my state of heightened awareness is to wake up, walk my dogs, howl in my mind at the moon, and say good morning to Mother Earth. I pray as I walk, I speak to the forces of nature to guide me through the day. I talk to the trees. I recite things for which I'm grateful. I ask how I can be of service to the higher good; that my life can be used as a vessel for goodness. This may seem like a lot, but some of these things are such fast re-sets that they take only seconds out of my day.

When I return from walking the dogs I sit in meditation for about five minutes and connect to my heart and to 'God'. Some of those times I light incense. Other times I have a morning coffee with reishi. I add the ritual of a daily elixir-smoothie, expressing gratitude to the plant medicine that I am about to ingest. As I evolve I'm sure my rituals will too.

I still have a goddess bath most days. And I write each day, as it is a source of calm and a creative outlet for me; it aids my balance. Crafting food is also an every-day event which is firmly entrenched in an all-encompassing ritual of gratitude, sustenance, and life-enhancement.

Food, for me, is one of those "mini practices" that have become sacred rituals that, on days I'm bordering on feeling overwhelmed, is the first ritual to go out the window. And after that the domino effect follows. Food, for me, is a non-negotiable self-care ritual because it informs me of my levels of self-care and balance. It's as invasive and loud as a dual signal railway crossing: lights, barriers, and sirens. You'll learn your own warning signs too.

Rituals connect me to myself and enable me to show up better in service for my life's work. I am grounded and sane because of them.

The more I find the highest expression of self, the less I am able to abandon it. In becoming more sensitive I'm less able to check out.

Life is a sacred, conscious ceremony. Living is a practice of rituals.

You are a precious human, billions of years in the making. Show up for short, doable, pleasurable appointments with your 'self'.

If you have ten minutes:
Take a walk, kiss the sky, bow to the earth, marvel the wonder of your body moving across space and time. Keep it simple, walk five to ten blocks without music and challenge yourself to notice five things per block that you are grateful for.

If you have one hour:
Abandon all to-do lists, and simplify by doing nothing, going nowhere: just be—without watching the clock—no agenda, for an hour. If that's hard for you, that's

okay, do it anyway. Ride the resistance, become curious and compassionate; not all things are easy to do at first.

If you have an afternoon:
Review what rituals you already have in your life. Do you make tea every day? Find a way to improve that routine by pulling out a treasured cup and saucer.

Decide what negative practices have let go—maybe you didn't even realize they were rituals.

Physically move things in and out of your space to support self-care rituals.

CHAPTER VI

Appendix of Rituals

THE WONDER OF each of us is our uniqueness. The rituals which nourish you will be slightly or completely different than those which will comfort, heal, or transform another person. A few basic rituals to tailor to your own life—ones that are known to benefit all (or most) of us are:

Gratitude

The moment one is capable of feeling grateful for pain and pleasure, without any distinction, without any choice, simply feeling grateful for whatever is given, simply because one knows all pleasure and pain it delivered for our growth, is an astonishing one filled with clarity.

Once this concept—an epiphany of sorts—settles in the heart, then each moment of life is one of gratitude. Existing in a constant state of thanks will bring about great peace in your heart and soul.

The practice of seeking out gratitude that strengthens our ability to feel and see more to be grateful for. Gratitude does not only show up in the sunny perfect days, it is to be found in the dark storms if we can only stop and look. Gratitude is unconditionally present—like the heart, it beats without our conscious recognition. Gratitude is a gift for us to tap into, literally, whenever we want.

A challenge for you: read this challenge then put this book down. Pull out a piece of paper (or write in the margins of Atlas of Darkness if this is a paper book), and write down 200 things you are grateful for. The stars, your mother, your health, the green grass, a job, a warm house, a car that gets you from point A to point B, a smile from a stranger, a special gift from a loved one, the ability to read, your functioning lungs, a heart that beats, seasons that are predictable, tears (for it means that you can feel emotion), school, dancing, music, summer, ice-cream, love, lessons learned, swimming, birthdays. Go - go - go, get your list of 200 before reading ahead. This way you'll have already started a ritual of gratitude.

Make gratitude a practice. Every morning, when you wake, state three things for which you are grateful. Start a gratitude journal. Gratitude doesn't mean that you have to put a smile on and pretend that you are not hurting. No, that is so not what gratitude means. Gratitude means that you can acknowledge your pain, you can authentically feel as a human and understand there is growth in each experience—essentially a silver lining. Find your silver lining.

Prayer

Find something to pray to. Something that marvels you, something that takes your breath away. Perhaps it will be God, perhaps grandmother Moon, a Hindu Goddess, or the miracle of cellular division. Find something to marvel over.

Be humble in your smallness and yet excited in your potential. Practice faith; the simple and simultaneously complicated practice of faith. Believe you are where you need to be right now in this very moment. It does not mean that you will be here forever, but it does mean that, right now, you are here. You are here and worthy and on purpose. Your life matters to the whole. The whole would be incomplete without your presence and your purpose (even if you don't know what your purpose is).

A daisy will become a daisy regardless of where it grows. Some daisies push through cement, others grow seemingly effortlessly on the forest floor. But each is still a daisy. Each harnessed the power of nature and surrendered to life in order to live life.

You, will be a 'you' no matter how you choose to grow or what environment you choose.

It is safe to believe in something. It's really okay to let go and marvel at a bigger picture. Look to the stars and simply surrender to this cosmic web of existence. Look at the mycelium of our Mother Earth's mushrooms, if you need an object of worship—this might just be it: mycelium.

There are so many things we cannot explain, so choose to marvel. Find something to pray to.

Journal

For as long as humans have existed, so has storytelling. The documenting of our own thoughts, desires, and feelings is invaluable to a healthy mind.

Go on a quest to discover the perfect journal for you. Do the same for a pen. Then start writing. There is no prerequisite for journaling. No rules. Just let the words spill out. No one will be correcting your grammar, or checking to see if your thoughts are in the right order—there is no order—there are only words. Your words. Your precious, sacred words.

Journaling is detoxifying. If you struggle with commitment, set a timer for three minutes each day and write anything that comes to mind. Keep them as a record to reflect, or burn the paper and send it back to the earth which will allow the great void to assist your cosmic journey.

Journaling daily is like tending your garden; it's like natural rain for your plants. It's like a glass of pure water for your psyche.

Healthy bowels - release

Adding flax, high-quality vegetables and fruits, and pure water to our diet helps us have healthy bowel movements. Healthy bowel movements are imperative to ridding the body of toxins. Bowel movements cleanse. It is the small intestines that are the main hub of digestion; so much assimilation and digestion of nutrients happens in this permeable spot in our human body. What is needed is kept, assimilated and transported to appropriate body systems, and what is toxic, wasteful, and unneeded is packaged up and sent to the large intestine.

Just as journaling is cleansing for the mental and spiritual metabolism, maintaining healthy elimination detoxifies and cleanses. Embrace this valuable bodily function.

Heal old wounds

We cannot run from our own shadow. We cannot run from ourselves, for wherever we go, there we are. We have got to place healing on the top of our priority list; we simply must look at wounds and figure out how to heal them.

We have to find a way to see our wounded selves in the light of compassion and offer the most radical forms of self-nourishment that we can think of.

Suppressing, numbing, running, hiding, blaming, ignoring and denying will only drive us further into discontent.

Be brave, your wounds are begging you to see them so you treat them. Consider therapy, engaging with a coach, or reading inspirational works on the subject.

Vital to healing is to work every-single-day on what you wish to be healed—not by dwelling on it, but with proactive thought and movement. One way to do this is to experience and 'feel the feels' that show up. Learn to honour the anger and tears without judging them. Commit to valuing the entire human spectrum of emotion, not just the ones you "like".

Letting-Go

We cannot carry all of the baggage we accumulate, it simply becomes too heavy.

We must, for our sanity's sake, learn to let-stuff-go.

This comprises the unfairness-es, the unjust actions of the world, the broken hearts, the hatred, the self-sabotage.

Letting it go does not mean we excuse the actions; letting it go simply means we free up some weight so we can fly at higher altitudes.

I carried the death of my father around for 26 years before I decided to look at it and work on letting it go. The anger and fear of abandonment poisoned me, ran my adult show, haunted my relationships, and kept me closed off.

I have worked, and continue to work, at letting go: therapy, writing letters, burning letters, tears, painting anger pictures—you name it I've done, and do it, daily. Praying to him, talking to him, wishing he was here, wishing him well, sitting on his gravestone and telling him about my day. Do whatever it takes for the soul to digest and let go of life's wounds.

Letting go does not mean erasing feelings, but it means not dwelling on past pain. Surprisingly, letting go means facing it head on. Wildly facing whatever baggage or barrier is there. We feel it, we stare it in the eyes, we wrestle it, and then we watch it crumble. Just as we eat flax to cleanse the bowels, we must find practices to cleanse our soul.

Role play with a stronger you, a future you, that can inform you how to let go of certain heavy boxes and suitcases. Refuse to see yourself as a victim. Drop the drama. Seriously, drop it. Be proactive. Run your life instead of running from it. And please, for the love of all things, give yourself the space to feel this process. It's the only way through.

Forgiving Others

This is a very heavy topic for me because my practice has been—after I've been hurt—to simply cut someone out of my life and then harbor deep resentment and sadness. The irony, hey? Who does this sort of behavior hurt? Certainly not the other human. It's like taking poison and expecting the other person to die. It doesn't fucking work.

You will have your own journey of forgiveness and your own examples. I am not in your shoes. I can only share the journey of forgiveness in my own life.

Specifically, yes, I have forgiven 'him' (PH). Yes, undeniably it was a struggle.

After I managed to get out and see clearly, I was so busy self-protecting and sorting my own life out that I could not see the collateral damage that this relationship had on me. And that damage was intense.

As I slowed down and faced my breaking heart, I developed a rage towards 'him' (PH); sheer hatred.

I hated him for the perceived wasted time. That damn thing stole three years of my life, or so I thought. I was mad for the insane reactions I had when I was around him. I was a fucking psychopath around him. I could not get my shit together if my life depended on it. I was dramatic and sulky and victim-ey. I carried around the words he called me in a 'basket of anger' (and, no, it is not becoming, *but I was proud of it*). I wore them like badges of honour—the Purple Heart for drama, the George Cross for victimhood: worthless, useless, dirt-bag. I was unable to shake those words from my soul; they were pinned to it and made me bleed. Until I could forgive, they continued to stab me.

Hating him only hurt me. Forgiveness allowed me to transcend into light. When I forgave, I began to remember who I was. I met my divinity.

Forgiving, just like letting go, does not mean condoning certain actions. Forgiving is a choice: freedom. Sometimes this freedom comes easily and other times it's a painstaking uphill battle. Sometimes I forgive and then find myself back in resentment again, burned by anger, suffocated by regret, smacked by riotous indignation. It's a journey, there is no finish line and, on the hard days where the old darkness creeps in, I keep it as simple as possible, notice it, nourish the self and the heart, and always engage in self-care.

I urge you to spend some time defining what forgiveness is for you. I promise you the freedom you receive from reaching a point of forgiveness will not compromise your boundaries. In fact, you will be stronger.

Resting

Oh, resting. This notion was foreign to me; it felt unproductive and lazy, and furthermore, once I rested it allowed the surfacing of all of the feels that had been pushed aside in the name of keeping busy. I would have rather done anything but rest. Rest, for me, was restless mind-hell.

But, alas, life has a plan in place for those who will rest. And when life demands we rest, we must. If we do not, if we resist the rest, we are into exhaustion, breakdown, fatigue, and/or sickness.

Wayne Dyer talk about "Minding the Gap", and he explains that the gap is sort of equivalent to the spaces between words; if we did not have these spaces, we would not have language, poetry, or communication. I liken this metaphor to music, without the space between notes we would simply have unrelenting noise—no melody, just noise.

The rest, the 'gap', the void, you see, defines all of what we do; without it our lives become a continuous noise.

Rest is an essential nutrient, just like Vitamin C, water, or fats. Without rest, our soul garden shrivels, and then she dies.

Rest is not lazy. Rest is not unproductive. Please, do yourself a favor and revisit your paradigms around rest. Ask yourself, 'what is the strength in rest'? Schedule your rest, practice your sleep, have reverence for your dreamtime. Your soul needs it, your body demands it, and you, Sister, deserve some down time... regular, down time.

Celebration

Take the time to celebrate all the milestones—each of the tiny shifts you've embraced. Party-up the culmination of your rituals. Pause and take notice of how was you have come.

Can you see that you are showing up moment by moment in the best way that you know how?

Are you different today than you were yesterday, or last week, or a year ago?

You are new and you are changing and you are soul-work in progress. Cut yourself a damned break.

Celebration is a key ritual, it is the fuel that motivates us, encourages us, pushes us forward to the next simple step. We cannot expect the self to respond with enthusiasm if we lash out at her with berating and difficult demands and expectations all the time. Look close and find the reasons to celebrate. No excuses here. Balls out: find them.

If you cannot see yourself through the eyes of your tribe, your sister, a coach, a loved one, or a stranger, then stay on that mission. Turn the tables and view yourself from the perspective of another.

Replay the tape of how you have been speaking to yourself. Then take another step forward.

Go out on a date, play, escape to the forest to blow bubbles, or go to the zoo, journal and reflect at how far you have come, write yourself a love letter, send yourself flowers, or get outside and pick some flowers, twigs, and branches to place on your altar. Do whatever it takes to recognize yourself. Cultivate your ability to celebrate, for recognition—self-recognition—has potential beyond your wildest imagination.

Create your own rituals; your own guide according to your soul.

Contact me, or others in your tribe, to share those rituals. Don't be shy. Your input will inspire others.

CHAPTER VII

Slip-ups: Dealing With Crises

IT'S REALLY EASY to fall asleep at the wheel and neglect dedicated self-practice when everything's going well.

I used to see this all the time, years ago, when I worked in the weight loss industry. Women would come to see me when something dramatic had happened which related to their weight. For example, maybe they bent over and their pants ripped, or they could no longer fit into most of their wardrobe.

This kind of event fires the desire to make change—a tension that is an amazing fuel to drive us to the places we want to go. But, just like an orgasm, this tension-based drive can't last forever. It will either be released as you make positive change, or it will morph into a severe handicap in the way of myriad illness and dysfunction.

Humans are experts at numbing pain and accommodating discomfort—numbing out is a coping mechanism.

When the pants do not fit, the tension is high. This increases motivation to change. It can seem so powerfully-simple to be motivated when life is falling apart; easy to commit to stop drinking when alcohol has caused you to lose the one you love; obvious to seek therapy in your darkest hour. Yes, damned-firm and hugely-inspired to drop a few pounds to fit into your clothes.

Tension is an amazing motivating factor. But what happens when the tension is gone? What happens six weeks into a new eating regime when the pants fit and life is grand? That's when we fall asleep at the wheel. That's when we stop the rituals and dedicated care that we chose to engage in order to get to that success.

I did this a million times myself.

It was easy for me to be focused when I felt terrible. Monday morning after a weekend of booze and falling back into a bad relationship I had depression, regret, booze blues, digestive issues, a headache, and brain fog. It was natural for me to envision success, start fresh, and create a bunch of dedicated plans of detox—the tension was high and so too was the motivation to change. Each Thursday, when my mind was clear and I'd done daily check-ins with my heart, when I was well rested and deeply self-connected, I began to be too overconfident. Things were going so well I'd let down my guard; allow a few self-care rituals to fall by the wayside. This would spiral me back into the vicious cycle that had me falling down Alice's hole at lightning speed. And every time I reached a lower level.

I believe the most risky time in life is when life is going well. We get arrogant and cocky—and we mostly become complacent. We fall asleep and stop our dedication to ourselves and we become deeply vulnerable to old patterns.

My experience is that each time these patterns kick back in they are more dramatic and the collateral damage significantly worse. We gain more weight than ever, drink more booze than ever, or sink deeper into depression than ever.

For me, each time I slipped, I would plunge further into my own nightmare. It was as if my soul was saying, "I will make this lesson so difficult for you that eventually you will either 'stay awake' and care for yourself or die."

Once I recognized that I would die, I created an "emergency list". This list was at the bequest of my therapist; a go-to list of tools to bring me up and out of a dark hole. It was my lifeline when darkness overwhelmed me.

Accessing my emergency list was what I did when the powerful wave of human emotion overwhelmed me. Instead of numbing out, I referred to the reminder of specific 'tools' that nourished me.

I made the list when I was awake at the wheel. I learned while on my A-game. I understood that self-care is required through all of life—the dark times and, equally important, in the light times.

Self-care was the tool that enabled me to ride the ever flowing wave of life.

My emergency list was kept on my phone so I had access to it at all times.

It contained:

TO DO:

- visit Dad's grave
- find a tree to sit with
- slow down, find softness
- cry
- self check-in, self check-in, self check-in
- focus on it's okay… this too shall pass
- art
- cooking

TO TAKE (pick one or two):

- reishi
- passion flower
- milk thistle
- holy basil
- schiszandra
- rhodiola
- peppermint oil

Self-exploration and awareness – creating your own emergency list.

Design your map of the world. Be your own cartographer and explorer. Set out on a quest to find, date, and establish a divine relationship with the love of your life—you!

In one continues minute—sixty seconds you can:

Stand in front of a mirror and repeat the words 'I love you' at least 45 times.

In one dedicated hour you can:

Begin learning about unconditional love, loving the whole self, embracing 'radical self-acceptance'. Write down what that might look like—sketch out in pictures or words what a perfect day looks like.

Make a list of negatives—things that you want to eliminate in your life. Burn it. Write out a list of positives. Hold it and curl up with it and nap with it.

And then be patient, this is the work of the soul gardener; eternal slow steady patience. This is a practice, a journey, a 'one-foot-and-then-the-next' process. Remember, there is no finish line and no race. This work is done over a lifetime—it's a journey. So slow down, there is no rush.

In one enchanting evening you can take yourself on a blind date by:

Dressing up for yourself in whatever way makes you comfortable. Not looking at what you perceive are your imperfections. Creating a date with yourself that aligns with your values yet takes you out of your comfort zone. Wine and dine yourself. Corsage yourself. Woo your own divine self. Date the goddess that is you.

And then do it again, and again, and again. Do it consistently, for all of your days on this earth. **All the Love, All the Days.**

Keep getting to know your ever evolving radiant self. Hold her when she needs you. Celebrate with her when she needs it. Your job is to fiercely protect her, love her, know her, understand her, and be her shoulder-to-shoulder best lover in the world.

CHAPTER VIII

Never Say Goodbye

I SAW A shaman in 2016, many moons after I left the negative chapters of my life. She told me that part of her vision included a bright light leaving my body. She believed it to be a male guardian leaving my adult-self in a way that was not 'departing forever', but that the guardian was letting go of his role as a guide as I no longer needed him. She further explained (without knowing any of my story) that this male guardian spread his wings over my life as a guiding force when I was a little girl. He wanted to be sure that I had protection and would learn to embrace the masculine and feminine.

I have no doubt at all that was my Father.

I also learned that my spirit animal is a stag.

The Stag is a powerful masculine medicine animal who emanates vibrant Yang energy. He represents vitality, confidence, pride, leadership, wisdom and fatherhood. He is intuitive—connected to nature. He is also said to represent regeneration, guidance, gentleness, healing, psychic power, independence and strength.

Growing up, I never wanted to get married, nor did I ever dream of having children. I wanted fierce independence. I dreamed of being an international speaker and a writer, and I wanted that success to be my very own—to prove to the world that I could do it, and I shunned the idea of asking for help or working with another human as a team. As well, I did not want love or a husband—it was simply never something I wanted or dreamed of. The more I loved, the more open I became to personal and professional pathways. That which was inflexible in me softened.

Looking back, I can see clearly that the desires I had were rooted in absolute fear. Fear of loss, fear of abandonment, fear of the uncertain nature of the world we live in. My fear was rooted in resentment. Resentment to God, about my Father dying, and generally directed to the overall 'un-fairness' of it all.

The medicine of the stag speaks volumes to me—however, in those days, before I even knew the stag was my spirit animal, before I had developed abundance through rituals of self-care, I was so completely out of balance that most of the beautiful qualities of stag and of divine masculinity had become overbearing shadow qualities.

The Shaman in 2016 told me that she saw two visions of me.

One was a vision of me with long blonde hair, and a fire: I was a witch and being burned at the stake. She told me that I was a powerful woman with attractive features. She said that I was not afraid, and she used current vocabulary in describing that I basically 'took one for the team'. Apparently someone needed to make a statement and I offered myself. I was killed for being a witch, for being an intuitive and powerful healer; for being a woman with a voice.

The next vision was me as a milkmaid. Again, she told me I was a strong and attractive woman, but circumstances meant I was at the mercy of an estate owner and he raped me.

These visions that she shared with me resonated deeply as this was certainly not the first time I'd heard this. I had been told by another intuitive that I was a witch, yet I'd been told I was an unattractive one and that I was wrongfully condemned to death, and succumbed to death via a gas chamber. I have been told numerous times by another one of my favorite intuitives that I was a woman in Atlantis.

Believing in past lives is not the point I want to make—what matters is how this 'woman with a voice' resonates in my soul. In the past, in this lifetime, being a woman has not felt safe to me. Until I began to understand my soul, my purpose, and to value my role, I did not feel safe enough to speak my truth.

The following observations serve as interesting points.

True or not, the messages-readings from the Shaman resonate and have helped in my healing journey to let go of fear. I have been able to see the bigger picture and to embrace forgiveness in a profoundly moving way.

I do believe in sacred contracts.

What I believe is that we are all capable of learning to provide an extremely safe place from which to speak; a sacred place to originate our voices and share our passions. We all need compassionate and unconditional love from ourselves before we can truly accept it and offer it to others. We require an environment that nourishes every cell in our bodies in a welcoming and comforting way, and we can each participate in relationships that serve the whole. We each deserve a soul that serves us as a soft landing space for the times we fall.

To become a whole and healthy individual requires that we dedicate time to establish rituals which will support our falling in love with the self. I believe with all my heart in 'you' because I believe in me. In order to embrace true love into our lives we must become the beacon of light for our own selves.

Through that love I believe that we can forgive. Can we forgive everything? Everyone? Of that I am not sure. But I do know it is possible to forgive oneself, and reflect on all that has happened in the past.

I am not an expert on you. I have become an expert on myself. I can say that, whatever you have gone through or are going through, one thing is certain: when you get to know what makes you shrink, your soul will always be on alert to remind you that you are ignoring your duty to love yourself. Each time you ignore, you will fall on your knees and begin to drop deeper underground.

Basically: when you know, you can never pretend you don't.

To be 'off balance in life' is disorienting. My Uncle explained it to me like this:

Think about a mobile that hangs above a baby's crib. If one of the pieces were to fall off, the entire mobile shifts and leans to one side. This is what happens in the self and also in group dynamics, such as a marriage or a family. When one piece shifts, the whole mobile has to adjust or just hang there off kilter.

Adjusting to repair the damage to the self, and within relationships, is not always pretty and requires a deep sense of self, boundaries and strength from a person who consciously chooses to show up for life in a new way.

This shit ain't for the light hearted, folks.

I have only been there in my own muck. I don't know exactly what yours is like. What I can say is that in my lowest times, my one saving grace was my dog. Such grace and power have all the creatures on the earth.

Maybe it sounds stupid, but my dog was all I had to live for in certain moments. I had a job to take care of him, and the visions of me lying dead and having him sit there with me, hurt me worse than the pain I was in.

Find your lifeline and hold on tight in your times of despair.

One of my very best friends in the world recalls the fear she felt from the texts I would send her. Seemingly, no matter how dark we become there is a tiny voice that can communicate with our fellow tribe members and say "help me! I am here. I need help". Reach out.

I am sorry for so many things that it would take another book to list them. Perhaps you are sorry for things too. Being sorry is a thumb-tack on a map. A visitor's spot. We are meant to move on to the next stage. We are, of course, at times, meant to make amends where we can, and acknowledge our roles while cleaning our side of the street, but forward march we must. Forgiveness.

I forgive all of where I was back then, because I know now that 'back then' I simply didn't have all the information about me. All the love.

We are not at fault when we don't know how to care for ourselves. We don't always understand, at first, that we are heading into the darkness. We can't always recognize the 'no entry' signs that can save us from a hell on earth.

I forgive myself for comparing my life to others and never feeling like I measured up. I forgive myself for disrespecting my body.

I look in my eyes today and I mourn for the woman I was. I weep for the mess she was in. I feel compassion today for her outbursts of anger, her deep feeling of isolation, and her hustle to fit in. I hold space for the fact that she did the best she could with what she had.

And I picture you. And feel your beating heart. And I hold space for you.

No matter how fucked-up we are, we show up. We do the best we can. We survive and, when we open ourselves to love, we thrive.

If I could go back in time to the woman I was I would offer her unconditional love and non-judgement. I want to tell her that I see the effort that she is putting in, that she is in fact not alone and that her future-self is so fucking proud.

I would explain that I now understand that at the age of six she began a journey of hope and healing that comprised years of dysfunction and produced a phenomenally resilient woman who is filled with wonder and love.

With all my heart, know that there is nothing to be ashamed of and there is everything to be proud about. I know that for me. I work on that every day. No sleeping at the wheel.

With all my heart, I want that for you.

Epilogue

THEY SAY LIFE is what happens when you're making other plans. Well, life happened as I prepared to read the final manuscript of Atlas of Darkness.

The same week this work was pronounced finished, and required only one more read-through, my life was turned upside down and inside out, without warning, by a shocking revelation, absolute devastation, and substantial emotional collateral damage.

Uprooted.

The essence of where I had placed trust and known love, suffered massive injury. Devastated, my world began to collapse and I was challenged to surrender to the deepest state of faith I have ever experienced.

I placed the project on hold—very temporary hold—mainly because it took all my energy to function. In hindsight 'project on hold' allowed me to see if I could walk the talk I'd written about.

The fact that you are reading this now, is proof that I could, and did walk the talk. I handled life by feeling all the feels, and accessing the dignity Mother Earth had provided me. Yes, I cried. And, oh! how I ached. So painful were all of those feels that I wondered if I'd be rendered lifeless. But I was not. I held my faith and surrendered—and did it sober.

Ironic, isn't it, that the timing of this book's completion, when I thought all was stable in my life, circumstances shook my foundation and attempted to render me a ruin?

The support I received from healthy relationships I'd formed was intensely comforting. The tools I'd used, then shared with others, and written about in this manuscript, worked for me so that I could process the darkness with a solid grip on my value and worth. Put simply, at the end of writing the manuscript I encountered circumstances I'd never imagined, then became my own experiment and used the self-help guide.

I made choices that did not compromise my standards, even though I was in shock. I did not shrink. I hurt like fucking hell, but I navigated because I knew how. It was as if an ultimate test was required to be the seal of approval of this book.

I thought having composed this book, in which I share my experiences of darkness and my initiation into using rituals to see the light, was enough to help myself and others—and, to a certain extent, this is true. However, the events that took place and temporary delayed the book's birth, was itself the ultimate test of mastering the loving rituals I'd created, and experiencing their power, and understanding their necessity.

About the Author

Kori Leigh Hagel is a teacher, coach, and nutritionist. She applies the holistic approach to her work and her food-crafting company, Farmapothique. Hagel also offers online classes and retreats, including A Course in the Rituals of Self-Care and Tribe for a Year.

In her new book, *Atlas of Darkness*, Hagel shares the long road she traveled after surviving abuse. Her past experiences inspired her to help others learn the practices of self-care and discover how to embrace the darkness.

Hagel lives in Calgary, Alberta, with her two dogs.